Fa

D1460512

Fashion has always been a competitive industry. As the pace quickens in an increasingly competitive business environment, effective marketing strategies are the key to success for couture houses and high street stores alike.

Fashion Marketing presents for the first time a comprehensive introduction to the main factors underpinning fashion marketing. All the main topics, from fashion PR to planning, range development to pricing and distribution, are explained clearly, supported by up-to-date examples from a range of sectors within the industry.

International dimensions are taken into account, with a focus on the impact of recent changes in Eastern Europe and the single European market. Encompassing an analysis of current social, economic and technological trends, the volume ends with a look ahead to the future of fashion marketing.

Providing key summaries and discussion points to aid learning, this text will be a vital resource for students of fashion and marketing at a variety of levels. Those working within the fashion industry who wish to understand the important area of marketing in fashion and to gain a sense of the wider picture will also find the book of great interest.

Janet Bohdanowicz is Senior Lecturer in Marketing at the University of Greenwich Business School and also holds a lectureship at the University of Warsaw. **Liz Clamp** is Enterprise Manager of Croydon College.

Fashion Marketing

Janet Bohdanowicz and Liz Clamp

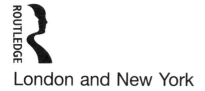

London and New York

First published 1994
by Routledge
11 New Fetter Lane, London EC4P 4EE

Simultaneously published in the USA and Canada
by Routledge
29 West 35th Street, New York, NY 10001

Typeset in Times by J&L Composition Ltd, Filey, North Yorkshire
Printed and bound in Great Britain by
Biddles Ltd, Guildford and King's Lynn

British Library Cataloguing in Publication Data
A catalogue record for this book is available from the British Library.

Library of Congress Cataloging in Publication Data has been applied for.

ISBN 0–415–05939–9 (hbk)
ISBN 0–415–05940–2 (pbk)

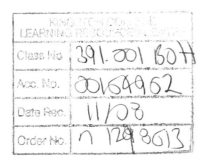

Contents

Illustrations

Preface

Marketing plays a vital role in the fashion industry. This is reflected in the growing number of fashion courses that contain a marketing or business element and marketing/business courses that include fashion retail modules. Students on BTEC, ND, HND, HNC and their G-NVQ equivalents and BA courses will find this book particularly useful.

Most students needing to acquire a knowledge of fashion marketing are faced with textbooks primarily intended for pure business or marketing students. Naturally, these deal with a range of manufacturing and service organizations which share only some of the problems faced by the fashion marketer.

The books and materials on fashion marketing are limited and they fall into two camps: those dealing with the American market and those that deal with the problem of industry-to-industry marketing. Some elements of the US-based material are useful but this material deals with a completely different marketing infrastructure. UK material focuses heavily on the interface between the textile and clothing manufacturing industries and largely ignores the ultimate destination of their product, the consumer.

Our aim in writing this book is to present all the basic marketing concepts within the context of the fashion industry. All of the examples and data in this book have been drawn from the fashion industry.

Adam Smith stated that 'the purpose of production is consumption', and the focus of this book is fashion marketing from a consumer perspective. As the consumer (the ultimate focus of the fashion industry) is beginning to understand more about the industry itself, a greater understanding of the consumer becomes vital for students studying fashion marketing.

Growth in the UK fashion industry has been sporadic and spontaneous to date. It has relied on the brilliance and innovation of individuals, be they designers, such as Mary Quant in the 1960s, manufacturers like Laura Ashley in the 1970s, or retailers like George Davies in the 1980s.

There is nothing to compare with the infrastructure for ensuring growth and stability that exists in the French fashion industry.

The creation of the British Fashion Council and the numerous fashion shows and data sources that have emerged reveal that the UK industry is trying to re-establish itself in world terms. This book is intended to make a small contribution to this change as the UK industry realizes that fashion means business as well as art.

Chapter 1

Introduction to fashion marketing

INTRODUCING THE FASHION INDUSTRY

The fashion/textile industry is the fourth largest industry in the UK today. Since the Industrial Revolution, the manufacture, wholesale and retail of clothing has been important to Britain as a source of income. Over the same period the French have developed their fashion/design abilities.

In the nineteenth century Britain rapidly expanded its textile manufacturing base to become a world leader – it was said that 'Britain's bread hung by Lancashire's thread'. Throughout this century, however, the industry has been forced into decline. There have been two main reasons for this: first, because Britain had colonies, it was able to use the resources of those countries (cheap labour and materials) for manufacturing. As the British Empire went into decline the former colonies began producing goods at prices with which Britain could no longer compete. Second, the involvement in both the First and Second World Wars meant that many clothing/textile factories were used for the production of munitions. Britain came out of the Wars with a huge national debt which meant that the money required to invest in new technology necessary for the country to compete in world markets was not available. Consequently, outdated equipment resulted in an increasingly declining industry.

As Britain's large manufacturing industries have fallen into decline, the service industries have increased and expanded. This is true of the retail industries and in particular the fashion retail industry. A number of reasons can be put forward to explain this: an increase in wealth; new technology; cheaper imports and a widening interest in fashion. However, it is the use and development of marketing that is mainly responsible for the expansion in fashion retailing.

Until the 1960s fashion was something your mother wore or it was the preserve of rich, older women as only they could afford it. Public taste was led by a few designers usually operating from Paris. As Anne Price, ex-fashion editor of *Country Life*, explained in an interview for the *Guardian* (23 February 1984):

> In those days we were reporting one look, the look. That was what fashion was about. Women all over the world waited to be told whether they should chop two inches off their hem lines and that story on the front page actually sold newspapers.

The look would then take three to four seasons before it reached the high street. There was at this point not very much choice with regard to off-the-peg clothing, and this was often purchased at either department stores or in small independent stores.

In the 1960s this all changed rapidly; names such as Mary Quant and Biba ensured that Britain became the place for fashion. Young, innovative designers began creating a look that had not only youth appeal but was accessible in terms of where it was sold and its price for the working teenager. Carnaby Street and the Kings Road in Chelsea became fashion havens and there was a huge spread in the development of fashion retailers with the advent of shops like Chelsea Girl, Dorothy Perkins and Foster Brothers. This new British look had international appeal. Unfortunately, it was not to last for long. Many of these new designers were enticed abroad, and as the industry itself did not take design or designers seriously, fashion again became dominated by Paris.

The British look did leave behind a design culture particularly amongst the young. Britain is known for its youth fashions and it continues to produce innovative designers. It also has an education and training system in place to promote this talent. Where Britain has always lagged behind its European, American and increasingly its Far Eastern counter-parts, however, is in its failure to understand and adopt marketing strategies.

THE MEANING OF MARKETING

Marketers are seen as preying on people's weaknesses in an attempt to force them to buy goods they neither want nor can afford. Unfortunately for marketing managers, the rails of remaindered 'bargains' at sale time or the failure of retailing ideas like the Woolworths womenswear collection demonstrates that marketers cannot coerce their customers into buying. They can only respond to customers' needs and wants within a given social and economic context.

In the fashion industry in particular, many of the myths about marketing are exploded. Let's look at some of these myths before arriving at a formal definition.

Marketing is just another word for advertising.

Many firms have just discovered to their cost that advertising alone cannot sell products that people do not want. Indeed, some very successful businesses in the fashion industry use advertising very sparingly, The Body Shop being a prime example. Advertising is just one of the tools available to the marketing manager to communicate with potential customers.

Marketing means selling – usually hard selling.

This myth depends for its survival on the idea of the totally passive customer. Once again, the fashion industry provides ample examples of cases where it is not possible to use sales pressure to make customers buy garments against their better judgement. When the Burton Group was setting up the Principles chain in the 1980s, its market research revealed that customers wanted friendly, helpful sales staff, but did not want to feel pressured into buying.

Many other myths abound about marketing. People still believe that designers and manufacturers simply need to make the garments and the retailer will do the rest. In other words, marketing is seen purely in terms of distribution. The UK Chartered Institute of Marketing presents a far more wide-ranging definition. It describes marketing as:

> the management process responsible for identifying, anticipating and satisfying consumers' requirements profitably.

Note that the focus of the management process is on the *consumer's* requirements. No matter how indirectly an organization has contact with the consumer, the consumer is the ultimate destination of the product.

This idea comes over more forcefully in a further definition of marketing:

> Marketing consists of individual and organisational activities that facilitate and expediate satisfying exchange relationships in a dynamic environment through the creation, distribution, promotion and pricing of goods, services and ideas.
>
> (Dibb, Simkin, Pride and Ferrell 1991)

So, in this definition we can see that all aspects of the fashion marketing process, from the conception of an idea to its delivery to the customer, come under the umbrella of marketing.

It is important to acknowledge the impact of the social and economic environment on the fashion marketing process, since few other industries are so powerfully and directly affected by social and economic trends. When the recession began to bite in 1991, fashion retailers, because they had felt its beginnings as early as 1989, were among the first to react to it.

The concept of a 'satisfying exchange relationship' is also of major importance. Marketing involves the exchange – usually of money, but also

Table 1.1 Marketing – the interface between the organization and its customers

Company	Marketing department		Customer
Resources	Marketing tools	Communication	
Labour	Product	Advertising	NEEDS
Materials	Price	Market research	WANTS
Capital	Place	Sales information	DEMANDS
Ideas	Promotion		

of time and effort, in return for goods. Sometimes people may be willing to invest more time or money in acquiring something that is highly desirable because they feel it has a greater value derived from its status as a fashion item. A fashion item is worthless when it is no longer fashion, as value is implicit in the item being fashionable.

At the heart of the marketing concept is the appreciation of the need to satisfy customers' needs, wants and demands.

NEEDS those basic human requirements for warmth, covering and social status;

WANTS implies the choices that a customer will make in order to satisfy those needs;

DEMANDS those wants which the customer is able to pay for.

Marketing can best be described as both a business function and a business philosophy. A business philosophy which places the customer at the centre of the organization's activities; a business function which is responsible for acting as an interface between the customer and the company, finding out about the customer and marshalling the company's resources to match their needs.

INTRODUCING THE TERM 'FASHION'

Fashion is inextricably linked with social trends; it does not just mean clothing but also accessories, cosmetics, footwear, even furnishings and architecture. The breadth of the term is reflected in the definition given below, which describes fashion as:

> a way of behaving that is temporarily adopted by a discernable proportion of members of a social group because that chosen behaviour is perceived to be socially appropriate for the time and the situation.
>
> (Sproles, quoted in Curran 1991)

This definition highlights two of the distinguishing features of fashion: its social role and its transience; and both of these have important implications for marketing which will be discussed in this book. Although the span of the term 'fashion' is very wide, in this book the focus will be on clothing, since clothing epitomizes many of the fashion issues that dominate the industry as a whole. The definition we favour for this purpose is given by Annalee Gold (1976):

Fashion is the dress that is currently adopted.

WHAT DIFFERENTIATES FASHION MARKETING?

The factors that differentiate fashion marketing from the marketing of other types of goods and services can be broadly classified into three areas:

- Strong influence of environmental pressures
- Time constraints
- Role of buyers

The marketing environment is examined in more depth later in this chapter. However, at this stage it is important to note that because of the social role of fashion, marketers operate in a far more complex environment than their counterparts in, say, fast-moving consumer goods. Two issues that particularly affect the industry are the international nature of the business environment and the complexity of the industry's structure. Some companies are fully vertically integrated like Laura Ashley and the French company Clayeux, and others, such as Charnos PLC sell through intermediaries.

The transient nature of fashion means that marketers must constantly operate within time constraints. The underlying factor is that the fashion industry moves with the seasons and that there are two main collections: autumn/winter, which, because of the British climate tends to be the best selling time, and spring/summer. There are also the mid-seasons and the Christmas/cocktail and cruise/swimwear collections.

The time-scale within which the industry operates is even more tight now; movement of designs from catwalk to high street has become so fast that there is a danger of them becoming outdated before they reach the intended store. In addition, technological developments mean that designs can be faxed across continents and cheap copies of designs can be available before any particular style has time to enjoy a period of exclusivity.

At the end of the 1980s there was a frantic search for a new look; something to take designers into the 1990s. Rifat Ozbek in his 1989 collection took the fashion design world away from matt black – his antithesis to this was a collection produced in pure white. This New Age look received rapturous applause from both public and press and the idea was seized upon by a high street heavily hit by recession and desperate to entice the shoppers back. New Age had become Old Age before Ozbek's own collection had reached the designer shops. Fashion marketing planners therefore have to respond to opportunities within time constraints. They also need to be keenly aware of any changes in the environment that may affect the business.

Lastly the role of the fashion buyer, which is dealt with in more depth in Chapter 7, has a key influence on the fashion marketer's job. While marketers are expected to respond to opportunities in the environment and to plan promotions and distribution, the job of the buyer is simply to select those garments that will generate the most profit and will best reflect their store's image and 'business mission'.

HISTORICAL DEVELOPMENT OF MARKETING AS REFLECTED IN THE FASHION INDUSTRY

Marketing has developed over the last three centuries as a response to the increasing gap between producer and consumer brought about by the Industrial Revolution. This development of marketing in industry as a whole has followed the pattern below:

Table 1.2 The historical development of marketing

Stage of development	Industry response
Pre-Industrial Revolution	Craftsmen and women working with close links to their customers, e.g. shoemakers, potters.
Production era	Customer satisfaction is sustained by improving production capacity, and making goods available at even lower prices.
Selling era	Production is surplus to requirements, so the focus is on selling with heavy use of promotions.
Marketing era	Effort is made to understand the customers' needs and tailor the products offered to them.
Societal marketing	The organization seeks to ensure that the customer is satisfied, in a socially responsible way.

Note: The development of off-the-peg clothing and greater accessibility of fashion during the past thirty years corresponds to that of the 'selling era'.

The fashion industry has not followed this pattern of development exactly. There are a number of complex historical reasons for this, which continue to have ramifications for the fashion industry as a whole, and fashion marketing in particular, to this day.

In the early 1980s, fashion retailers became more marketing orientated, developments such as Next and Principles were successful because they made great efforts to find out what customers wanted and tried to give it to them. The use of electronic point of sale (EPOS) systems, enabled companies like Next to track which items were selling well and ensure that supplies of popular items were readily available; slow-selling items could also be highlighted and quickly withdrawn.

The 1990s could be seeing the emergence of the 'societal marketing' concept in the fashion industry. The increasing popularity of 'recycled' clothes and the use of 'green' production methods for textiles are indicators of this movement.

THE CHANGING MARKET ENVIRONMENT

The changes that take place at national and international levels will always have consequences for industry. Fashion is particularly susceptible to changes that take place in the business environment. As in any business, the factors that will have the greatest effect can be summarized as:

Political
Economic
Social
Technological   **(PESTEL)**
Ecological
Legal

The marketing department needs to monitor each of these factors on a continuous basis in order to anticipate how they will impact on the business. Although each of these factors will have a different effect on each individual organization, it is worth discussing the type of effect each of these factors has on the fashion industry as a whole.

Political

Politics will affect both the producer and the consumer in various ways. Political activities have a powerful effect on people's moods; the strong ideological drive towards private ownership in the 1980s not only saw business expand at a rapid rate, especially in the retail sector, it also precipitated a desire for conspicuous consumption and aspirational dressing, as people bought clothes which reflected a more affluent lifestyle, for example, the increase in the design and production of the business suit.

International political events have even wider ramifications for the fashion industry. The single European market has put the UK fashion industry under pressure to compete on several fronts, both in terms of design, manufacturing quality and production costs, as it has broadened the field of competition.

The collapse of communism, while presenting opportunities for such companies as Littlewoods, which has made a great success of its stores in St Petersburg, has also posed a threat in the form of the availability of cheap labour and cheap textiles much closer to the European market than other competitors in the Far East. Of course, the threat posed by war to supply lines cannot be ignored either. Early in the war in the former Yugoslav Federation, consignments of shirts from Serbia for Marks and Spencer were halted.

Economic

The fashion industry is international and is therefore strongly affected by international economic issues as well as by national economic problems. Trade agreements, such as GATT (General Agreements on Tariffs and Trade) dictate the role exports will play in an organization's marketing plan. The effects of exchange rates also need to be monitored closely; the devaluation of sterling in 1992 led to a rise in the cost of imports to the UK while making manufactured items more competitive. The economic factors which have the greatest effect on fashion marketing are inflation and the availability of consumer credit, which stimulates buying. Cutbacks in the purchase of items considered to be non-essential such as fashion garments are often the reaction of consumers during recession.

Fashion itself is often seen to be affected by economic cycles, for example, the often remarked upon link between women's hemlines and the state of the economy has been noted by fashion historians and journalists alike. This states when times are good, hemlines go up, as in the 1920s and 1960s, and when times are bad they go down, as in the 1930s and 1970s. Given today's fashion (which is no longer dictated – there is not a 'look' to follow) and people's attitudes in general (they favour more individualism and are more likely to buy a garment because it suits them than because it is fashion), this theory no longer holds true in the 1990s.

Social

There have been many developments in habitat as a result of changing family structures. Several general trends emerged out of the 1991 census. Young people no longer feel pressure to be married or have children, and therefore many are living a single life or are cohabiting. The stigma once attached to single mothers has been largely removed and this, coupled with a higher rate of divorce, is creating more single parents. As divorced parents remarry taking children from a previous marriage with them, this results in a new form of family. Children in further and higher education are staying on longer 'at home' financed by parents.

Many of the changes have been helped by a demographic profile that began to change many decades earlier. In the 1960s two things were to happen which would affect childbirth patterns. First, there was the invention of the contraceptive pill and second, the availability of free contraception given by the new Family Planning Clinics for both married and single women. The passing of the Abortion Bill (1967) also had an effect, if only because it was further legitimization of a woman's control over her fertility. By the mid-1970s the effects of these changes were becoming apparent in nurseries and schools. It was not long before retailers noticed and in the 1980s began to look for a new market.

Those people who were born between the end of the Second World War and the start of the pill were to become known as 'baby boomers' due to the massive population increase. At the end of the Second World War the government actively encouraged a return to 'traditional' family values. The effect was not just to try to stabilize a nation but to give jobs to men returning from the War and also to increase the population. The situation has been termed 'the pig in the python'. This baby-boomer generation was to benefit from increased educational and healthcare facilities. Those born at the end of the 1950s represent an important group to the marketers and they have become known as the 'thirty-something generation'. Their importance lies in the fact that there are so many of them and that they have proved to be willing consumers.

Many of the baby boomers have or are beginning to have their own families. Yet they have a great desire to remain young, and this has led to the redefinition of the term 'young', which can now mean 25–44 years old. In the mid- to late 1980s this audience was provided with fashion. It could be argued that the term 'fashion' too has been reworked for them. The increase in the number of working women began to have a real impact on the fashion industry in the 1980s. Designers such as Donna Karan and Giorgio Armani found markets with those who wished to dress for success. Next provided career women with a designer look repeating this message of dressing for success but at high street prices. Fashion moved out of today's teenage market back to the grown-up teenagers of the 1960s and 1970s.

This wider and more youthful outlook has many implications: to be young is to be doing and to be doing is to be achieving. If middle age is set to start at 44-plus then those who are at retirement age cannot be considered old. Whole industries have been set up to provide for the new market often referred to as the 'grey market'. Members of this group are affluent; they wish to have a full role in society and all their lives have had ready access to fashion items. They are unlikely to stop a lifetime's habit of spending now.

Plate 1.1 The *Clothes Show* magazine (photograph: Wendy Carrig)

Changes in social values are also changing the output of the fashion industry. Increased interest in sports and leisure has been reflected in the increased popularity of sportswear and training shoes as fashion items. The huge impact of the 'green movement' has also had an impact on fashion, as we discuss later in this book. Its most noticeable effects have been on the manufacture of textiles, and the allied animal rights movement has led to the almost terminal decline of the fur industry.

Technological

Technological change affects both production methods and the choices made by the consumer. CAD/CAM have had enormous effects on the manufacturing sector, while EPOS has changed the face of stock control for retailers. While technology brings many benefits for UK manufacturers, it is a constant challenge for marketing management to keep abreast of changes.

Technological changes have had a great impact on the daily lives of consumers. The ready availability of audio-visual technology has led to the development of TV clothes 'magazines' like The *Clothes Show* and to videos of fashion shows being commonplace items. Thus the consumer is far better informed about developments in fashion than ever before. The technology of clothes care – washing machines, driers and steam irons – also make caring for clothes much easier for people thereby broadening their choice of fabrics and so on.

Technological developments have also meant that international competition is even fiercer. Designs can be faxed direct to manufacturers in the Far East where they can be made for much less than it would cost in Europe and samples can be flown back by courier in much the same time as it would take for samples to be sent from one end of the UK to the other.

Ecological

Our understanding of the environment and the impact of human activities on the ecological support system is constantly developing. Ecological considerations play an important role in marketing activities, particularly in communications. For example, ecologists have questioned the use of natural fibres because of the great cost to the soil caused by ill-thought-out irrigation methods such as those used in former Soviet Central Asia and the widespread damage caused by over-use of fertilisers in parts of the USA. This new understanding of ecological issues has led to the return in popularity of synthetics. Courtaulds, for instance, has been developing some new synthetics which have been used by the Label Clothing Company, Frank Usher and Monix in some of their designs. The problem for the marketing manager is convincing customers that man-made fibres can be better for the environment than natural ones!

Even the distribution of fashion clothing can have ecological implications. Road transport accounts for 85 per cent of total carbon emissions and the fashion industry accounts for a significant percentage of road haulage. Designer Katharine Hamnett now uses pedal-cycle couriers and railway transport where feasible.

Legal

International and national legislation impacts on the way in which fashion companies trade. Revision of Sunday trading laws in the UK could lead to an increase in consumers' levels of discrimination in purchasing, rather than an actual increase in sales. With more time to choose, shopping for clothes will cease to be a hurried lunch-time affair for most working people.

The impact of EC legislation on clothing will be even more profound; fiscal legislation will standardize the amount of VAT levied on clothing throughout Europe, for example. Standardization of clothing sizes is also likely to affect the market.

These examples do not even begin to consider the myriad other legal regulations, such as the Trades Description Acts, which the marketer must consider when formulating advertising messages or employment legislation which can affect the labour forces of large manufacturers and retailers.

BRIEF OVERVIEW OF THE STRUCTURE OF THE FASHION INDUSTRY

The fashion industry has been discussed in most of this chapter as if it were a single, homogeneous industry. It actually consists of a multiplicity of different industries which all interlink with one another. Fashion marketers at all stages of the fashion industry chain (Figure 1.1) need to be aware not only of the other industries they are involved with but of the ultimate destination of their products, the consumer.

Some companies are vertically integrated. Burtons, for example, was totally vertically integrated – 'from sheep to shop' – before their restructuring. Courtaulds is partially vertically integrated, since it produces dyes and fibres and is now also involved in clothing manufacture, and Laura Ashley has both retail and manufacturing arms.

The complexity of the marketing task in the fashion industry is enormous. Technological changes have meant that elasticity of demand in the retail sector has a much faster knock-on effect on manufacturing than it did a few decades ago. The development of marketing in the industry has not been homogenous; while one part has become more responsive to consumer demands, other parts have tended to lag behind. The effect has

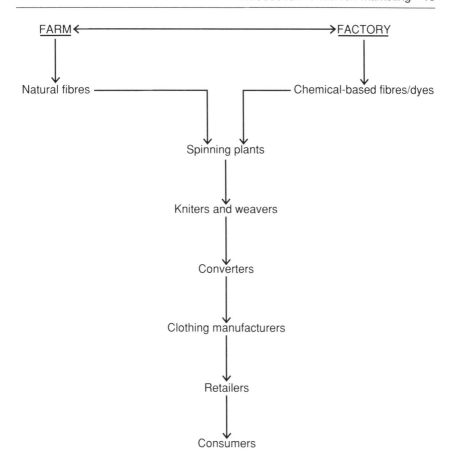

Figure 1.1 The fashion industry chain

been largely negative for the UK fashion industry, since retailers have been sourcing more and more from overseas. The current move towards more institutionalized assistance for the fashion industry, which has been spearheaded by Sir Ralph Halpern's creation of the Fashion Council, may redress some of this balance.

The marketing mix remains central to the marketer and this book will examine the four P's:

- Place
- Product
- Promotion
- Price

Chapter 2

Consumer buying behaviour

INTRODUCTION

We have already identified the fact that fashion is essentially a social phenomenon. Fashion transcends the basic human need for warmth and protection. It provides individuals with a statement of their identity and affects how the individual relates to others both within a given group and within society as a whole.

The study of consumer buying behaviour in the context of the fashion industry is therefore an extremely complex process and one which the marketer needs to grasp fully in order to develop a successful marketing plan. Adoption and diffusion theories explain how particular styles evolve, but other factors converge to precipitate the purchase of a particular item. In this chapter we will examine the consumer both as an individual and in relation to social groupings and society as a whole. We will also evaluate the consumer's decision-making process and how the fashion marketer can use knowledge of this to assist in the marketing of fashion products.

Consumer buying behaviour theory draws heavily on the work of psychologists, sociologists and social anthropologists. In an international context, social history also offers important insights into consumer buying behaviour, since we need to understand the cultural background of another country or region if we are to be successful there. It is an accepted truism that even international brand-name clothes like Wrangler and Naf Naf will be worn differently by, say, an Italian and a Scot.

CONSUMER NEEDS AND MOTIVATION

Satisfying customer needs and wants is the primary task of the marketing-orientated organization, whichever part of the fashion industry it is in. If it fails to do this, it is out of business. Human needs extend beyond basic physiological drives, they also provide the consumer with the motivation to buy. Understanding the motivational drives can help fashion designers and marketers alike to target their products more effectively.

Maslow's hierarchy of needs

One of the classic explanations of human motivation was developed in the 1930s by the psychologist Abraham Maslow. He postulated that people have a hierarchy of needs, and until one level is satisfied, other levels will remain unsatisfied.

Figure 2.1 Maslow's hierarchy of needs

The hierarchy of needs is not a cast-iron law, like the law of gravity, but it provides a useful starting point for understanding and discussing the range of motivational forces behind the consumer's purchase of an item of clothing. Of course, we can immediately note that fashion consumption does not always correspond to this model. Most consumers will seek to satisfy physical needs for warmth and comfort before worrying about other factors. While this may hold true in times of crisis or in subsistence economies, in developed economies different levels of need frequently prevail. Conversely, the need for social acceptance or enhanced self-esteem causes people to suffer in the cause of looking good, for example, Scarlett O'Hara's agonies in having her corset tightened.

The needs, as suggested by Maslow, are explained below:

- **Physiological needs**   These would prompt the purchase of a winter coat. Of course, someone who had no means to satisfy that need, like a homeless person, could not afford to have fashion considerations and would wear any coat given to them. This basic need could also spur a product search, in the case of a more wealthy customer, which would involve other levels of need being satisfied.
- **Safety needs**   These relate to both physical and emotional safety, although this may in general be a minor issue for fashion marketers. However, some purchases will involve a high level of safety

consciousness, such as taking into account the flammability of children's nightwear.

- **Social needs** Examples of this are the need for acceptance by our families or by our own social group. Social needs can exert a powerful influence on fashion purchase, as is exemplified by the complex issues involved in the teenage purchase of sports shoes. We will be discussing social needs in more detail later in this chapter.
- **Esteem needs** This implies the need for recognition from others. Prestige or the wish to enhance our reputation is a motivating force across the whole fashion spectrum, from street fashion to haute couture.
- **Need for self-actualization** This is often interpreted as the expression of creativity or some type of spiritual fulfilment. The fashion marketer can observe this motivational force at work in both the creative dresser, whose whole appearance is a well-thought-out design in itself, and in the 'consumer with a conscience' who would shop at Lynx and Oxfam as an externalization of their beliefs.

McClelland's trio of needs

Some psychologists, McClelland foremost among them, believe that there is a group of three basic needs which provide the mainspring for human action. Those which provide the drive or motivation for purchase in the fashion consumer are: need for power, need for affiliation and the need for achievement. These needs, which are explained below, can be closely related to those in Maslow's hierarchy.

- **Power needs** These relate to the need to control one's environment, including other people. At various times, power needs can be seen to have an effect on fashion, epitomized, or perhaps parodied, in the 'power dressing' of the 1980s, as exemplified by shoulder pads and sharply tailored suits. Certainly, where an individual has a need to exert power or authority over others, clothes are often seen as a necessary adjunct to the exercise of power.
- **Need for affiliations** This need is a well-researched social phenomenon which exercises considerable influence over customers' buying behaviour in a range of ways. First, there is the individual with a strong need for the approval of others, who may be influenced to buy a garment by the approval of the salesperson. It also includes those individuals who buy an item in order to gain approval or acceptance by a particular group, and can be seen in the unofficial 'dress codes' at workplaces, as well as more obviously in the social structures surrounding the purchase of brand-name trainers.
- **Achievement needs** These are similar in nature to the esteem and

self-actualization needs identified by Maslow. People with a high need for achievement are often motivated by the need to do something for its own sake. For such people, clothing purchases may be made in order to reflect those achievements. Appeals to this type of motivation can often be seen in promotional material for luxury fashion items: 'You've earned a Rolex', runs the copy.

PERSONALITY AS AN INFLUENCE ON CONSUMER BEHAVIOUR

Personality refers to those inner characteristics which will determine how each consumer responds to their environment. Trait theory, which ascribes buying behaviour to personality traits such as sociability, competitiveness, aggression and so on, has often been used to explain people's fashion buying behaviour in terms of the colours and styles selected.

Personality is also an important determinant of store choice; not only is there the question of achieving a match between the store's own personality and the customer's, there is also the issue of how different personality types may be catered for by different stores. Those who lack confidence in their dressing ability may prefer a store like Next, where co-ordinates are pre-selected, while those with plenty of confidence in their own style may select clothes from a number of independent retailers.

The problem for fashion marketers who wish to make use of the study of personality is that it is an extremely difficult variable to measure, requiring the use of trained psychologists to carry out the field work and interpretation of data. For designers then to interpret these findings may result in clothes that are not always accurately matched to customer requirements.

PERCEPTION

Perception is the psychological process whereby people interpret the things they see around them and come into contact with. It involves receiving, selecting and retaining information, and so it plays a very important part in how customers react to aspects of the product, such as the label, and other parts of the marketing mix, particularly promotions. Knowledge of the perception process is helpful in developing store, brand and product images, as well as in product positioning.

- **Selective perception** Fashion marketing managers need to pay special attention to the issue of perception when developing advertising campaigns. Most people are bombarded with advertising messages throughout the day, yet remember very few of them. The explanation lies in the way we perceive the messages. We screen out a lot of information that is not directly relevant to us. For example, if we are not contemplating buying swimwear and have no particular interest in swimwear design, we will probably not even notice an advertisement for say Slix swimwear when we are reading a fashion magazine; only when we are already considering making a purchase will the advertisement stand out. This is what is known as selective perception.

- **Selective distortion** This occurs when the person receives information with which they disagree, for example we would remember a garment which is advertised as being in a crease-resistant fabric if we have found that fabric to crease easily. In this case the advertisement will only have the effect of irritating the consumer.
- **Selective retention** This is a common experience for most people, when we remember some but not all of the points made in an advertisement, for example, we remember the setting or the earrings the model was wearing, but not the suit which was the whole point of the advertisement.

The personal characteristics of the consumer will have a great influence on the buying decision. In an introductory book of this type there is not enough space to give a full discussion of the issues involved; people who wish to examine the topic further will find a wealth of interesting material in texts on both the sociology of fashion and consumer behaviour. Some useful titles are given at the end of this book.

DOES CONSUMER BUYING BEHAVIOUR HAVE A RATIONAL OR EMOTIONAL BASIS?

We have examined some aspects of customer motivation, perception and personality and how these might affect fashion buying behaviour. Underlying any discussion on this topic is the issue of whether buying is a rational or emotional process. For the marketer, rational decisions would be those based on objective criteria, such as price and size, and emotional motives would be purely subjective, such as the desire for status.

While there is a very small minority of people whose buying behaviour is so driven by emotion that it has been identified as a specific behavioural disorder, 'shop-aholism' as it is popularly known, most purchasers bring a mixture of rational and emotional factors to their purchase decisions. Emotional motives, such as the need for social acceptance may propel a buyer towards the purchase of, say, Fila sportswear, but rational considerations such as price and fit will also play their part. The fashion marketer's job is therefore to understand the emotional driving forces and the rational constraints involved in buying fashion items.

DEMOGRAPHIC CHARACTERISTICS

Demographic characteristics will affect both the type of clothing that individuals will buy as well as exerting influence over rational choices which s/he will make.

- **Age**   This remains one of the main determinants of people's buying behaviour despite many demographic and social changes which have taken place, such as the slump in 'teenage' fashions.
- **Gender**   Also an important factor affecting a person's choice of clothing, gender remains important since there are very few genuinely unisex fashion items – even jeans are advertised as either feminine or masculine, e.g. Wranglers recent advertisement asks: 'Does our new range fit perfectly? Was John Wayne a cowboy?'
- **Occupation**   This has become an important influence on people's choice of clothing. Clothing can be chosen to reflect one's professional status or to indicate that one belongs to a particular occupational group. Bella Freud has designed clothes for female barristers to wear in court.
- **Economic circumstances**   These will dictate how much discretionary income is available to be spent on fashion items. Discretionary or disposable income is not as straightforward as salary, for example, the professional person with a high salary will be less willing to spend on fashion items if they have children to support. Included in this item is the availability of credit, which can affect the amount of money available to spend at any one time. Catalogues such as Freemans offer credit terms.
- **Social class**   Class is strongly linked to occupation and income, but it has far wider ramifications in terms of purchase behaviour, particularly of fashion items. For this reason, it will be discussed later in this chapter in the context of fashion marketing and the individual in society.

So far we have discussed the individual consumer, but the adoption of a particular fashion is generally viewed as a manifestation of group behaviour. Understanding how groups work and what their effect is can help fashion marketers to understand and predict patterns of adoption of new products as well as assisting in planning effective marketing and communication strategies.

REFERENCE GROUPS

A reference group is a group of people (or even one person) which provides a point of comparison or reference for the consumer in the formation of values and attitudes, which in turn affect buying behaviour.

A reference group can have a direct or indirect influence on a person's behaviour, depending on whether a person wants to show that they belong to a particular group or to dissociate themselves from a group or attitude. There are four main types of reference group:

- **Primary**
- **Secondary**
- **Aspirational**
- **Dissociative**

Most people belong to several if not all types of reference group.

- **Primary reference groups**   These are those groups with which the consumer has daily contact, thus they will exert a strong influence over selection of a large part of the consumer's wardrobe. Typical groups are fellow students, friends at work or even family members. These people provide a ready forum for discussion of purchases, in addition they have an important effect on choice – most people will adhere to an informal dress code at their place of work. 'Creative' organizations such as advertising agencies or design studios would expect those people involved in the creative part of the business to dress informally. One advertising agency which holds a large jeans manufacturer's account expects their staff to be wearing the jeans when the client visits.
- **Secondary reference groups**   This refers to formal groupings with which the consumer has less contact, for example, sports clubs and professional associations – a tennis club may insist on all whites. They will have some influence over fashion item purchases, since people will want to signal their belonging to a particular group, but their influence will be less than the primary reference groups with whom there is daily contact.
- **Aspirational groups**   These are of particular significance to the fashion marketing manager. These are groups that the consumer would like to belong to or aspires to. The influence of the aspirational group can be seen in the widespread adoption of fashion items worn by celebrities, for example, the lacey look that Madonna made popular. Particular social groups' 'fashions' are copied, for example, the filofax, once associated with the gentrified vicar, found a ready market selling to the 'yuppie' and others who aspired to that status, and it eventually filtered down and was widely copied by chain stores.
- **Dissociative groups**   Equally important are those groups whose values the consumer rejects. The effect of these dissociative groups can be seen in the way people dress to 'make a statement'. Punk, for example, was originally a statement of dissociation from commercialized fashion, although it was eventually commercialized and sold

back to the young as a fashion look. More recently the 'grunge' look made an anti-commercial statement although it is interesting to note that this fashion has been copied and sold to a much wider audience in terms of age and class than punk.

SOCIAL CLASS

Social class remains important to the structure of British society and despite the narrowing of social differences by education and job mobility it is still seen as a reliable indicator of people's values, attitudes and lifestyle. Like speech, dress is an important signal to others both of the social class we originate from and the social class to which we aspire, and as such it needs to be well understood by the fashion marketer.

Table 2.1 Social classes in the UK

Class	Description	Occupation
A	Upper/Upper-middle class	Higher managerial, administrative and professions
B	Middle class	Middle managerial, administrative and professions
C1	Lower-middle class	Supervisory/clerical
C2	Skilled-working class	Skilled manual workers
D	Working class	Semi-skilled and unskilled manual workers
E	Lowest level of subsistence	Pensioners, casual workers, state benefit recipients

The commonly accepted descriptions of each of the social classes are given in the above table. Although social class is accepted as an indicator of values and attitudes and is used by marketers to determine in which publications they place advertisements, there are several drawbacks which can make it unreliable especially for fashion marketing. Social class is usually decided by the occupation of the head of the household or chief wage earner, usually assumed to be male. This means that women's social class is often hidden, for example, a woman solicitor married to a primary school teacher will be allocated to social class C1 although she herself could be placed in social class B.

FAMILY

As well as being most individual's primary reference group, the family exerts a far wider influence over the individual's fashion buying behaviour. There are three main effects of the family:

- Joint decision making
- Consumer socialization
- family life cycle

Joint decision making

In many families, the purchase of an expensive fashion item such as a coat will be a joint decision, with parent, spouse or sibling acting as adviser to the person who will wear the item. The different roles that can be seen in the joint decision-making process are:

User   the person who will wear the garment;
Decider   this could be the wearer or the adviser;
Buyer   this could be the wearer or in the case of a young person another family member.

It is important when considering promotional plans, particularly personal selling training, to bear in mind that fashion purchase is not always a decision the consumer makes in isolation.

Consumer Socialization

'Consumer Socialization' defined by Ward (1972) as the 'processes by which young people acquire skills, knowledge, and attitudes relevant to their functioning in the market place', has an important bearing on the marketing of fashion today. Although most of the research has been conducted into the influence of the family on children's development as consumers of FMCG (fast-moving consumer goods), many of the findings are equally applicable to fashion marketers. The most relevant points of this process are the fact that children accompany their parents on shopping trips and learn how to select items, how to compare price and quality and how to match styles and colours. Today's young consumers are usually skilled shoppers by the time they are buying clothes for themselves and only those organizations that recognize the fact will be able to succeed in the market-place.

Family life cycle

The family life cycle (FLC) is a means of classifying the stages through which a family develops. It provides a framework for evaluating consumer behaviour, since the FLC provides some clues as to people's priorities and available income for family purchase.

An example of a family life cycle which has been based on the model developed by Murphy and Staples (1979) is given on the next page:

Table 2.2 The family life cycle in stages

Stage	Description
1	Young single
2	Young married
3a	Young single with children – under 5 – over 5
b	Young married with children – under 5 – over 5
c	Young divorced with children – under 5 – over 5
4a	Middle aged married no children
b	Middle aged married with children – under 12 – over 12
c	Middle aged single/divorced – children under 12 – children over 12
d	Middle aged married no dependent children
e	Middle aged single/divorced no dependent children
5a	Older unmarried – Single – Divorced – Widowed
b	Older married

The FLC provides some background information about stages in the development of the family when people might give priority to fashion spending; for example, as young single people and, later, when home-making and children's clothes become more of a priority. Grandparents today have greater spending power than before and research has shown that they are spending this disposable income. The FLC is a tool which assists in the evaluation of marketing and promotional plans.

THE CULTURAL CONTEXT OF THE CONSUMER

Culture is usually defined in terms of the external characteristics which distinguish one society from another: music, art, literature and clothing are all manifestations of culture. Culture is a set of learned beliefs and attitudes that are acquired rather than being inborn. Of all the factors which influence the buying behaviour of fashion, culture is the most complex, simply because fashion is an important aspect of culture. The advent of the single European market has made the issue of culture even more important for fashion marketers both in terms of what British manufacturers may be able to sell to other European countries and in terms of a development of a European-wide fashion industry.

Although national culture exerts a strong influence over the way in which people dress, it is important to realize that under the umbrella of national culture other sub-cultures operate which also strongly influence buying behaviour. The sub-cultures which have the strongest influence on fashion buying are:

- **Religion**
- **Ethnicity**
- **Occupation**
- **Generation**

- **Religion** Religious belief may influence fashion buying in terms of rules relating to modesty, thus many Islamic women will adapt European clothing to conform to the calling of their religion, opting for trousers and jeans rather than short skirts.
- **Ethnicity** Strongly linked to religion, ethnicity will impact upon buying in a similar way in that most Islamic people have their family origins in other continents. The other area in which ethnicity has a strong impact is in the powerful influence of black fashions on mainstream fashion in Europe and America. As Nicola Jeal, editor of British *Elle* magazine, notes, it is not only 'ragga' but a whole line of clothing styles that have been adopted by the mainstream culture, having originally been worn by one particular ethnic group, for example, Fred Perry tops and sunglasses.
- **Occupation** This will provide consumers not only with a reference group but in many cases they will subscribe to the culture of that occupation. This leads to the adoption of particular styles of clothing to conform to the image of the particular occupational group.
- **Generation** This will have a slightly different influence to age, in that we are looking at a group of people who have all shared the same historical experiences, for example, the over-60s, who have all experienced the rationing of clothing in their youth and will not see fashion clothing as throwaway items, unlike their children who grew up in the 1960s, for whom fashion buying became a hobby that has only recently been curtailed by the recession and family responsibilities.

Culture will affect product plans, the type, range and lines of garments that an organization will make. It will also have an important bearing on where the garments will be distributed – someone over 65 would not normally go into River Island for a skirt but would prefer more traditional outlets; likewise, 'streetwise' fashion is not normally immediately available in major chainstores. In addition, the type of promotions used and the media selected for advertising and PR will be strongly influenced by cultural considerations.

While the fashion historian or sociologist can afford to take a detached view of the topic, the fashion marketer must take an analytical approach and try to judge how these cultural factors will affect the total product offering.

THE FASHION BUYING DECISION-MAKING PROCESS

The process by which people decide to buy a fashion item is of key importance to marketers, it provides the basis for decisions such as promotion and distribution strategy. There are three basic phases to the consumer decision:

| Pre-purchase | Purchase | Post-purchase |

Pre-purchase stage

Most people's purchases are started by a trigger which could be an internal need, for instance for self-esteem, or an external factor – an item in a fashion magazine may draw a woman's attention to a new design. This trigger will lead the consumer to realize the existence of a problem or to recognize a goal they wish to attain, such as the purchase of a new sweater.

The next stage in the pre-purchase phase is the information search, where the consumer will draw on internal knowledge about styles, designers and specific stockists of clothing and external sources of information; for example, magazines or colleagues' opinions. The consumer will then evaluate the alternatives, based on predetermined criteria such as price, utility, colour, style and so on.

Purchase process

The basis of the purchase process is the exchange of money for goods. The marketer must make decisions regarding each of the factors which go to make up this process:

- **Place** Mail order/shop/type of shop/market stall/party plan, etc.
- **Time** Peak time (lunchtimes or Saturdays) or off peak – this determines the amount of attention the consumer will want from the sales assistants
- **Means of payment** Cash, cheque, credit card, storecard or instalments – the payment means will have implications for pricing and for post-purchase satisfaction levels.

Post-purchase phase

This phase is very important because it will determine future fashion purchases. At this stage the consumer will actually be wearing the garment and thus will consider levels of satisfaction. Consumers will also receive feedback from others in terms of whether the garment suits them and from items in the media which will serve to reinforce their decision. A customer may then gain reassurance from seeing a recently purchased item on a fashion page of a magazine.

SUMMARY

The fashion marketer needs to be aware of the needs and motivation of the consumer. To do this there are several factors which need to be taken into account:

- age/generation
- gender
- occupation
- economic circumstances
- social class
- religion
- ethnicity

The marketer also needs to observe the social and political climate. For example, in 1986 there was not a mass concern for the environment; by 1989 this had completely changed. A launch of 'green' clothing in 1986, therefore, would have had little relevance to the consumer and it would not have sold.

It is also important to understand the perception process. This mainly happens in the following ways:

- selective perception
- selective distortion
- selective retention

Finally, the fashion marketer must provide a level of customer care, for it is after the purchase that the consumer decides whether they feel they have made a good choice.

DISCUSSION POINTS

1 Take three different people of a similar age, profile them in terms of their demographics and suggest where they might purchase their clothing.

2 Take four different advertisements for clothing, analyse the advertisements in terms of how they appear to the customer and try to describe which sort of consumer would be attracted to the advertisements.

3 Go into a store on a busy shopping day, observe how people select and buy their clothes. If possible choose a store such as a children's store where more than one person is involved in the purchase and see who has the most influence.

4 A consumer is most nervous at the point of purchase, as they have still probably not decided whether the purchase is right, and indeed will not 'know' until the garment has been worn for an occasion. How would you help the customer to leave the store feeling good about the purchase and the store?

Chapter 3

Marketing research

THE IMPORTANCE OF MARKETING RESEARCH TO STRATEGIC PLANNING FOR FASHION MARKETERS

The satisfaction of customers' needs, wants and demands lies at the heart of the marketing concept. No organization can afford to rely solely on intuition or guesswork as a means of finding out what those requirements are. Marketing research underpins the entire marketing effort. It provides a means of assessing the market in a logical, structured manner so that sound decisions can be made across the whole range of marketing strategy.

- **Product design** The fashion industry is often said to be design/ production led, rather than consumer led. Chapter 5, on new product design, demonstrates that the process relies as much on perspiration as inspiration; marketing research provides designers with vital information and feedback on which aspects of a particular garment are most satisfactory to customers. This information plays an important part in the design process.
- **Competitive management** One of the characteristics of the fashion industry is its vulnerability to environmental change. Fashion managers need to be constantly aware of developments in both the macro-environment (i.e., the PESTEL factors outlined in Chapter 1) and the micro-environment which means particularly current information on competitors, buyers and suppliers. Market research is the tool used to keep this information flow going and to use it effectively so that the organization retains its competitive position.
- **Manufacturing planning and sales forecasting** Developments in manufacturing management, such as 'just-in-time', coupled with technological improvements on the retail front, such as EPOS, have reduced the risks of producing large levels of unwanted stock. Nevertheless, accurate sales forecasting is still an important element in the fashion marketing process. Sales forecasts provide the basis for

most of the budgets, since estimated sales levels must provide the basis on which the management can predict the amount of materials and other resources required in the forthcoming production period. Sales forecasts are also needed by production managers to help them plan production schedules, and marketing managers can use them as a method of assessing and controlling the marketing plan. Marketing research plays a vital role in drawing up sales forecasts and will be discussed later in this chapter.

- **Pricing and distribution** In the fashion industry the value placed on a product is often related to the cost of producing it. Extensive research into consumer reactions to pricing is needed, therefore, before the marketing manager's final decision can be made. Closely related to the pricing decision is the decision of which distribution channels to select. Although experience plays an important role in such issues, marketing managers will need to back up their decisions with research.
- **Promotions planning** In the area of promotions planning particular care needs to be exercised in matching the right message to the customer and ensuring that the message is presented through media that actually reach the target customer. Marketing research provides the information on which decisions regarding such issues as media selection, sales promotion formulation and sales staff training plans can be made.

Top designers like Bruce Oldfield are in constant contact with their clients. Their situation is akin to that of the craftsmen prior to the Industrial Revolution. Personal contact enables them to find out exactly what the customer requires and to develop the product that will suit their needs. Formal market research is largely superfluous at this level of contact, but for larger manufacturers and retailers catering for a wider market it is vital. Marketing research is necessary to reach a full understanding of the customer and to ensure that the marketing planning process is structured and logical rather than a purely intuitive process which leaves the business open to lost sales through unanticipated environmental change and to competition from better organized rival firms.

THE BASIC CONCEPTS USED IN MARKETING RESEARCH

Understanding more about marketing research is important not only for those directly involved in fashion marketing but also for those working in all areas of the fashion industry who find it useful to understand more about how the information on which their work depends is gathered, which information will be more accurate or cost effective and the overall market research process.

First, it is important to distinguish between marketing research and market research. The two terms are not interchangeable but have entirely separate meanings. It is also important to understand what is meant by marketing information system or MIS.

- **Market research**   This refers to a specific one-off project for a particular purpose, for example, wearer trials of new underwear designs to ascertain which fabrics to use in final production.
- **Marketing research**   This is an on-going process, which incorporates specific market research projects but also embraces wider issues like competitor information and environmental monitoring.
- **Marketing information system (MIS)**   provides the framework within which all the information-gathering procedures and sources within the organization are harnessed in order to provide timely accurate information. The MIS is also known as the management decision support system (MDSS) since it is tapped into to provide information to support decisions in other areas of management besides marketing, for example, production and finance. The full workings of the MI System will be explained later; at this stage it is important to realize that although the marketing manager will be responsible for the day-to-day activities of the marketing information system, either directly or indirectly, s/he will often need to call on the expertise of an outside agency to provide the depth of knowledge required on specific issues.

When a marketing manager needs information on a specific aspect of the fashion market, take for example the issue of store location and design, s/he has a choice of two different types of marketing research information:

- **Tailor-made research**   The TMS partnership, among others, calls this one-off research. This is where research is done for a particular purpose, such as monitoring the performance of a particular store or assessing consumer attitudes.
- **Off-the-peg/Off-the-shelf research**   This refers to information which is gathered on a specific industry sector like women's hosiery; it can be used by a variety of organizations for various purposes. An example of this type of research would be the *Clothing Sales Index* (CSI) produced by the TMS partnership and giving details of sales trends, etc. in the clothing market. Marketing managers can use this information as a basis for their own market research planning.

SOURCES OF MARKETING RESEARCH

Marketing research essentially falls into two categories, depending upon the source of our information and data collection methods. The two categories are:

- **Primary research** This refers to information that is obtained direct from source, for example, information on customer attitudes used by the Wallis group for their product positioning is obtained by directly questioning actual and potential customers.
- **Secondary research** This is research carried out using sources of information already in existence. That is data which has been collected for some other purpose already; this could be a previous market research study into the topic, an off-the-peg report like the *Clothing Sales Index*, or government statistics such as household expenditure surveys.

Secondary research is cheaper and more easily carried out than primary research and is often undertaken first, but the information gathered by primary research, as it is more up to date and precise, is invaluable when making high-risk decisions.

SECONDARY RESEARCH

Secondary research, also known as desk research, is a term which embraces information already assembled for other purposes from a range of sources, both internal and external to the company. Secondary research is usually used at the start of a market research project to amass background information before the organization commits itself to more specific primary research. It is also a cost-effective method for a small company to use for assessing its market. For example, a company considering selling ski-wear in France will be able to use secondary data to ascertain the size of the existing market, those areas in France where sales are highest, the average 'spend' of consumers on such products and the strength of competitor firms in the area. This information would then allow them to decide whether a viable market exists for their products and whether it is worthwhile carrying out primary research to find out the precise requirements of the market. Secondary data is available in a variety of forms: hard copy, printed information, on-screen from on-line, CD/ROM and interpersonal services from libraries and trade associations. It can be obtained from both internal and external sources and will generally need to be interpreted by the researcher.

Internal sources

Most organizations hold a wealth of data that will be extremely useful to the fashion marketer; it is a question of getting hold of it and interpreting it. There are three main types of internal records which are useful:

- **Accounting records** e.g. invoices which give quantities bought;
- **Sales force records** such as reports from sales staff;

- **Management records** such as personnel records and production schedules.

External sources

For researchers in the fashion industry there is a huge range of data available which reflects the size of the task involved in monitoring an industry which is dealing with a complex market.

Government sources

The government produces a large amount of data which is an ideal starting point for an investigation into the consumer market for a particular product or for an assessment of an industry's competitive position. We have selected a list of those publications which will be of particular interest to those working in the fashion industry, but it is worth obtaining a free booklet entitled 'Government Statistics: a Brief Guide to Sources' produced by the Central Statistics Office (CSO) and published by HMSO, if you require further information. The main government sources which will be of interest are as follows:

- **Business monitor** published by the Department of Trade and Industry (DTI) contains data on topics like market trends and covers manufacturing industry as well as retailing and wholesaling.
- **Family Expenditure Survey** gives a regional breakdown of the incomes and expenditures of UK households and includes details such as the proportion of family income spent on clothing.
- **Social trends** is a compendium of information from a variety of government sources on various issues from birthrates to membership of voluntary organizations.

EC sources

The EC produces a range of useful information for those who want to do business in Europe. A variety of materials is produced on an *ad hoc* basis and there are two regular publications:

- *Bulletin of the European Community*
- *Economic Survey of Europe*

Commercial sources

A number of organizations carry out regular surveys of industry sectors such as women's clothing, footwear and hosiery. These are useful for gaining a broad understanding of the market. The most useful ones for market research in this area are:

- **Jordans** (surveys)
- **Mintel**
- **Keynotes**

For competitor information, such as the size and profitability of companies, the following sources are useful:

- **Dun and Bradstreet**
- **Kompass**
- **Business Ratio Reports**
- **Extel**

On-screen sources

The advantage of on-screen data is that it is quick to obtain and the use of a database that can be accessed by key words means that hours of searching can be avoided. Major on-screen sources that are readily available consist of two major types:

- **CD/ROM** information is stored on hard disc and it is updated periodically, e.g. ABINFORM or FAME for business information;
- **On-line** where there is direct access via the telephone system to a larger database, e.g. Prestel and Textline.

Many of the commercial information providers such as Jordans, and ICC (publishers of 'Keynotes' and 'Business Ratio' reports) now have on-line databases too.

Interpersonal services as sources

Most libraries will keep copies of major reports and government statistics, and many borough library services have also developed business reference collections. Some specialist business libraries, such as the City Business Library and the Science Reference Library in London, Birmingham Central Library and the main libraries of Glasgow and Cardiff, have a wider range of sources. Libraries of universities and colleges which run fashion courses will also keep material that will be useful to people researching a specific area of the fashion market.

Specialist sources

Trade associations and government bodies set up to assist industry can also provide useful information. Of particular interest to fashion marketers will be the British Overseas Trade Board, which can provide information and advice for those wanting to market their products internationally. The British Clothing Industry Association and the Fashion Council also offer information and advice for fashion marketers.

Market research agencies as sources

Market research agencies provide both tailor-made research and secondary research for their clients. Most of the 200 agencies listed by the Market Research Society as being specialists in the clothing industry have their own libraries and specialist researchers who can provide advice and assistance for companies with general or specific marketing needs.

PRIMARY RESEARCH

Primary research, otherwise known as field research, provides direct access to customers. Most primary research for large companies is carried out by specialist market research agencies, this is because the complexity of the task and the high degree of risk associated with incorrect information means that most marketing departments do not have the staff necessary to carry out the work.

There are two types of information that can be obtained from primary research.

- **Quantitative**
- **Qualitative**

Quantitative research will provide 'hard' information on which managerial decisions can be made, it will answer such questions as 'What percentage of men aged 15–21 watch "The Big Breakfast"?' which may prove useful if advertising'sportswear.

Qualitative information will be about customers' opinions and attitudes to particular issues, it is particularly useful for new product development and promotions development. Qualitative research would enable management to ascertain customers' reactions to a new fabric or method of payment, for example.

QUALITATIVE RESEARCH TECHNIQUES

These are two major methods of carrying out qualitative research:

- **Group discussions**
- **Depth interviews**

Group discussions

These are also called focus groups and consist of a group of six to eight people who will be gathered in relaxed surroundings, either someone's house or a hotel, where a trained facilitator will manage a discussion on a range of topics connected with a particular product. In this way, the feelings and opinions of people can be uncovered. However, the value of the information obtained depends on how the company interprets it; the company may choose to ignore the findings or interpret them in a way which fits their existing strategies, as in the case of a major US jeans manufacturer launching a range of ready-to-wear suits which flopped.

Depth interviews

These are one-to-one interviews, usually carried out by a trained psychologist, which seek to discover more details about individual's reactions to products or ideas. The depth interview is more likely to be used when products of an intimate nature rather than products in more general use are being researched, thus it may be useful for discovering people's underwear buying habits.

Qualitative research is useful when the company is probing the market, for example, when Courtaulds was developing a new range of textiles it needed to assess potential buyers' reactions; it can also be used to investigate people's reactions to the promotions programme. The main drawback of qualitative research is its expense, which is why it is used only for high-risk ventures, for example the revamping of Chelsea Girl into River Island required extensive research into the attitudes and opinions of potential customers.

QUANTITATIVE RESEARCH

Quantitative research results in information which is presented in numerical form. There are three main methods of obtaining data:

- **Observation**
- **Experiment**
- **Survey**

Observation

Observation can be carried out either in the 'field', for instance in a department store, or under controlled situations, like a market research agency's 'laboratory'. What it involves is trained observers noting the behaviour of customers as they shop for various items. This method of research is useful for understanding more about the customer's reactions to displays of clothing and to store layout. It is invaluable for tasks such as store design.

Experiment

Like observation, experiments can also be carried out either in the field or in the laboratory. The difference between observation and experiment is that in an experiment the researcher will control the variables, such as the product or promotional material. The most well-known form of experiment is 'test marketing', which involves launching a product or an advertising campaign in a restricted area and analysing the results before widening the marketing effort to other areas. Marks and Spencer's use of their Marble Arch store to test reactions to new products is a classic example of test marketing.

Survey

Survey is the most frequently used method of data collection, and involves obtaining information usually by means of a questionnaire (which is directed at a specific, limited group of people rather than the whole population, in which case it would be called a census). Naturally, it is seldom feasible to question everybody within a particular category – for example, all women aged 25–40 – so a sample is used. There are two main methods of selecting a sample:

- **Probability sampling** is where all people within a particular category have an equal chance of being selected. A probability sample (or random sample) would be taken for example by selecting members of a studio television audience. Each member of the audience would be given a numbered ticket and a computer would then randomly select say 10 per cent of the ticket numbers, who would then be interviewed. This is only a feasible method of sampling when we know the total number of people in the group (universe), or the group from which we are taking our sample, and when we have the means to select them in a truly random manner, uninfluenced by any human judgement.
- **Non-probability sampling** involves the use of human judgement in making the sample. The most popular method used, because of its cost effectiveness and simplicity, is the convenience sample. In this case, interviewers would simply select a number of members of, say, a television audience corresponding to 10 per cent of the total and interview them. It is known as non-probability since not everyone has an equal change of being selected for interview, such as someone who is temporarily unavailable at the time the interviews take place.

QUESTIONNAIRE CONSTRUCTION

This plays a vital role in the production of quality data. The subject matter of the questionnaire must be carefully considered and subjects must be grouped in a sensible, logical order. Attention must be paid to the order in which the topics appear. It is advisable to start a questionnaire with a non-contentious question to engage the participant, e.g. 'Is this your first visit to Debenhams?' Personal data, such as age, occupation and income group are usually left until the end of the questionnaire, since people are often reluctant to disclose such information and having these questions at the start of the questionnaire can lead to a rise in non-completion rates.

Care must be taken to phrase the questions in an unambiguous way, so that respondents are quite clear what they are being asked and so that it is easy to tabulate and analyse the data at the end of the survey. Broad, open-ended, questions, such as 'What did you think of Courtaulds' "Tencil" as a clothing fabric?' will elicit such a broad range of responses that analysis will be difficult. Usually, questionnaires will mainly consist of closed questions, i.e. those requiring a straightforward yes/no answer. One such question could be 'Have you bought a new jacket in the past six months?'

Likert scale

Respondents' views on, for example, product quality, can be obtained by using the Likert scale. This is where respondents are presented with a series of statements, such as, 'Clothes need to be easy to take care of', and a range of responses across five bands:

Strongly agree	5
Agree	4
Uncertain	3
Disagree	2
Strongly disagree	1

When the responses are added together, a high score would indicate that a large number of people feel that easy-care clothes are important. It is a relatively straightforward means of obtaining a variety of information.

Before a survey is carried out, it is important to conduct a pilot study, i.e. to test the questionnaire out on a small group of people to make sure that all the questions and any instructions are easy to understand and that the questionnaire is not unduly lengthy. Once the pilot study has been completed, the full-scale survey can be carried out.

Survey methods

There are three commonly used survey methods:

- **Personal interview**
- **Telephone**
- **Post**

The method used will depend upon the timescale in which the information is required and the budget available , as well as on the type of information that is required.

- **Personal interview**   This method involves interviewers approaching respondents and asking them questions from the questionnaire. The interview can be held in the respondent's home or in the street or in the store. The advantage of the personal interview is that visual aids, for example, fabric or product samples, can be used or, in the case of advertising research, examples of advertisements can be shown. Information can be obtained quickly and, if convenience sampling is used, a representative group of people can be interviewed easily. The drawback for most organizations is the expense involved and the fact that interviewers can actually bias the outcome of results, perhaps by assisting the respondent in the interpretation of a question. Interviewees can sometimes give responses which they think will please the interviewer. For example, a respondent who is not confident about their dress-sense could respond to the question, 'Is your appearance important to you?' with a 'No' answer simply because they feel defensive when confronted by an immaculately groomed interviewer.
- **Postal surveys**   These are probably the cheapest form of survey to carry out and are often used for consumer goods market research. For the fashion industry they are of limited and specific use because of the constraints of time and the low response rate. In a fast-moving business environment, surveys which take a total of six to eight weeks to carry out will be too slow, except for very specific, long-term projects. The low response rate (20 per cent is considered good for postal surveys, 10 per cent is more usual) means that the response may not be very reliable, especially for socially important fashion items.

For the fashion marketer, the most important requirements when carrying out a survey are for speed and accuracy, which frequently leads to the selection of personal interview as the preferred means of data collection.

Syndicated research

Although it uses primary data collection techniques, syndicated research is not carried out on a one-off basis. It is research which will be carried out by an agency on behalf of a number of clients in a given field (e.g. clothing retailers) who will share the cost of the research project. The types of syndicated research which will be of particular interest to people working in the fashion industry will be:

- **Consumer panels**
- **Omnibus surveys**

These two types of syndicated research are summarized below:

- **Consumer panels**   The panels consist of a 'resident sample' of consumers who agree to be interviewed on a regular basis about their buying habits. Research agencies tend to specialize in a particular field, for example, using panels of younger people.
- **Omnibus surveys**   These are questionnaires containing questions from a range of companies and are directed towards a particular category of respondent, thus a man might find himself being asked a range of questions, from the type of shampoo he uses to where he would purchase a pair of casual trousers, in the same questionnaire. TV ratings, which measure by using a meter or by immediate interviewing the programmes people watch, are of some relevance for scheduling advertising, but will not be needed on the same regular basis as they are in the food industry. Likewise, retail audit can provide some useful information about sales of some items, but it is more useful in product areas where there is less differentiation between the goods.

ORGANIZING THE RESEARCH

Finally, we need to examine the process which is involved in carrying out market research. If we take the example of a company wishing to research the market for men's fashion socks we will notice that the following process is used:

1 **Definition of Research problem**
   What information is needed, what is the research objective?
   To find out who are the main purchasers of men's fashion socks, the potential size of the market, outlets at which they will be purchased and purchase occasions.
2 **Outline sources of information**
   Secondary sources will be used for the initial appraisal of the market, but primary sources will be used to provide additional data.
   Internal records may be used to ascertain existing markets for the socks, general surveys on the hosiery industry and on consumer spending, e.g. CSO (Central Statistics Office) publications will be used, followed by interviews with a sample of men and women aged 20–40.

3 **Data Collection techniques**
How will the data be collected?
Personal interview will be used to collect data quickly.

4 **Collection of data**
Where and when will data collection take place?
Data will be collected in store, during the hours of 12–2 when many workers shop during their lunchbreak

5 **Data processing**
Data will be collated and analysed, some responses will be cross-tabulated for additional insights.
Data processing will be facilitated by the use of computers to process and tabulate the data.

6 **Communication results**
Presentation of oral and written reports.

You will note that once the initial appraisal of the market has been made, the focus of the research is on primary sources of information.

THE MARKETING INFORMATION SYSTEM (MIS)

The MIS provides a means for the fashion marketing manager to harness all the information resources at his/her disposal, so that they are accessible for management purposes. An MIS can be computerized, or it can be hard copy (i.e. entirely paper based), or a mixture of both. The important fact is that a system exists whereby information is gathered by the marketing department and processed into a system which will allow it to be used to assist in decision making.

A small company manufacturing ladies gloves will need to gather information from internal sources, external sources like trade journals, and industry reports and trade associations, in order to keep abreast of developments in their sector. The information bank can then be used to monitor opportunities for growth, competitor movements and environmental threats, such as rises in business taxes which will affect profits.

A typical MIS will have inputs from:

- **Trade magazines** like *Drapers Record*;
- **Internal sources** like sales records;
- **External reports** like *CSI* (Clothing Sales Index) and *Fashion Monitor*.

It will be used to provide information useful for:

- **Monitoring** sales of new products;
- **Identifying** market opportunities;
- **Tracking** competitor activity;
- **Preliminary research** for market research projects.

SUMMARY

This chapter examines:

- The importance of marketing research for fashion marketers;
- The role of marketing research in both planning and design;
- The difference between marketing research and market research;
- The Marketing Information System, and how it assists marketing planning;
- Secondary research, the data sources that are especially important for the fashion industry researcher;
- Primary research, how the different data collection methods can be used by fashion marketers;
- The market research process.

DISCUSSION POINTS

1 You have been asked to conduct marketing research for a proposed independent store which is to set up in your high street. What research would you undertake to do this and how would you go about it?
2 Devise a questionnaire around a particular fashion garment, show colleagues an illustration of the garments and try to access how popular it would be and where to sell it. Remember to ask about quality, colour, size, care, etc.
3 Another European company is about to establish a chain of shops in the UK, they would like to undertake research first. What sources would you advise them to use?
4 Organize a research programme for a children's wear clothing company wishing to expand its range to include children's shoes. Develop a strategy for determining its success among present customers.

Chapter 4

The international dimension of fashion marketing

MAKING SENSE OF THE TRENDS IN INTERNATIONAL FASHION MARKETING

Fashion marketing can be differentiated from other types of consumer marketing by the level of internationalism which exists within the industry. This level of internationalism can make things very straightforward – garments can be exported to an overseas distributor – or extremely complex, as is the case with Benetton, a large, vertically integrated operation. The changing shape of Europe has intensified the impact of the international environment and will form the focus of our discussion in this chapter.

Understanding the underlying framework of international marketing operations in the fashion industry and the effect of the international business environment on fashion marketing is of key importance to everyone in the fashion industry. It enables us to evaluate the competition for our products and to assess new markets. Without this analytical approach, the fashion marketer can find her/himself merely selling, rather than marketing the ranges, thus losing ground to the competition.

An analytical approach to fashion marketing is particularly helpful in making sense of some of the debates which arise within the industry from time to time, such as whether we are moving towards a standardization of fashion designs and marketing within Europe. It also helps to decide on ways to cope with profound changes such as the re-emergence of Central Europe in the market economy.

In this chapter, we will examine the different ways in which international fashion marketing can be approached; we will then look at the constraints and opportunities afforded by the international environment. Finally, we will examine the practical issues involved in researching and planning fashion marketing operations in an international context.

APPROACHES TO FASHION MARKETING IN AN INTERNATIONAL CONTEXT

International involvement exists in various forms throughout the fashion industry, if we accept Terpstra's (1987) definition of international marketing as marketing activities which are performed across international boundaries. The very wide range of involvement in international marketing which exists within the fashion industry is demonstrated in Figure 4.1 below.

Approaches to international marketing within the fashion industry vary from casual exporting, as a result of over-capacity for example, through to the global orientation of a firm such as Levi's. What each of these approaches entails will be discussed in the following section.

Exporting

Fashion companies can have varying levels of commitment to international marketing, from casual to committed or active exporting.

- **Casual exporting**   This is exporting at its lowest level. When fashion companies do not actively seek export markets as part of their marketing strategy, exports tend to happen 'accidently'. For instance, a small shop owner on vacation may decide to buy in a range of garments on a one-off basis. This is known as casual exporting.
- **Committed or active exporting**   This begins when the fashion company makes active efforts to market their goods overseas. In the

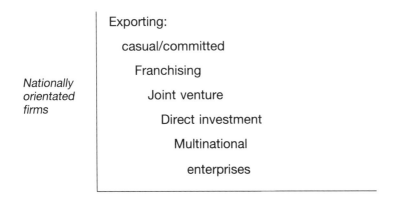

Figure 4.1 Approaches to international fashion marketing

fashion industry, there is plenty of support from both government and trade associations for companies who wish to be involved in export markets. The Department of Trade and Industry (DTI), through the British Overseas Trade Board (BOTB), and the British Knitwear and Clothing Export Council (BKCEC) provide help for fashion companies wishing to research the market as well as ample assistance in promoting products and companies through such events as the 'British Fashion' exhibition, which runs in Japan on an annual basis.

Fashion companies which have a commitment to export marketing will make some adaptations for different markets, producing smaller-size ranges for the Japanese market, for example. Promotion and pricing will be done through the large exhibitions and fashion shows, and pricing will be dependent on the form of distribution adopted.

Franchising

As we will discuss in Chapter 6 on distribution, franchising arrangements are an increasingly popular method of conducting business overseas, since this approach requires very little capital investment.

Licensing

Closely linked to the franchise idea is that of licensing. In this method of doing business internationally, the fashion company sells the use of assets, such as a logo or designs, to other companies. Used carefully, this can be an excellent source of extra revenue, but sometimes the overuse of a particular designer label can devalue it, losing a great deal of its core business. This is what happened to the Pierre Cardin label in the 1980s, where overlicensing resulted in too many poor-quality garments being marketed under the Pierre Cardin name, with a subsequent loss of prestige customers from which the company is still trying to recover.

Joint ventures

Another way in which fashion companies can gain access to new markets, or more economical methods of production, is by the joint venture. A joint venture is a form of business partnership where two or more organizations share in the ownership of a direct investment. The joint venture is proving to be a useful means for EC fashion companies to gain a foothold in the Central and East European markets, and also to fend off competition from the Far East by gaining access to low-cost production facilities. Poland has many joint-venture companies in operation now, and almost 20 per cent of these are in the fashion industry. Swedish, German and American firms dominate this area because of their historical and geographic links to the country.

Direct investment

By owning shares in a foreign company, the fashion company can gain access to other markets or resources. Companies hoping to take advantage of growth in Eastern European markets in the long term are investing there now, either through share ownership or through investing in technology, as Adidas has done in Hungary.

MULTINATIONAL ENTERPRISES

There are two major types of multinational enterprise that dominate the international fashion industry: the multi-domestic company (confusingly this is frequently referred to as the multinational, or just the international company) and the global company.

Multi-domestic

This type of company will operate across international boundaries, but each country's operations will be independent, with most management functions undertaken by the country's nationals. Retailers will have different store formats in each country, and local management will control product mix, pricing and promotions. Sears Holdings (the US-owned retail giant) is a good example of this type of organization; it owns the fashion store Miss Selfridge in the UK.

Global

The global fashion company integrates its operations in different countries and designs and markets its garments for a single segment world-wide. Fashion companies producing 'commodities' such as jeans and trainers have been very successful with this approach, many other types of garment have not proved suitable for a global manufacturing and marketing strategy.

   In the fashion retail sector, global retailers tend to be those which offer the same type of merchandise to the same target markets in each country (e.g. C&A, Laura Ashley). Andre Tordjman of the Centre HEC-ISA (Hautes Études Commercials – Institut Supérieur des Affaires, in France) noted the three key characteristics of the global retailer:

- **Classic, or fashionably classic merchandise**
- **A unique merchandise offer**
- **Own label merchandise**

Many global retailers were vertically integrated companies which also controlled their own production and design, such as Benetton and Laura Ashley. Global retailers also tend to have a centralized marketing system, and to exercise strong control over local marketing management.

Deciding what form of international marketing to adopt will depend on:

- Organizational objectives
- Potential growth in the market
- Size of the competition
- Business environment risk

Many Far Eastern firms have the objective of gaining market share from domestic-produced goods, and tend to export at very low prices; British firms such as Marks and Spencer wish to improve their organizations' overall financial performance, so they go for direct investment. Many organizations are interested in entering the former communist market, because although returns may be low at the moment future prospects are good.

THE INTERNATIONAL BUSINESS ENVIRONMENT – CONSTRAINTS AND OPPORTUNITIES

The major distinction between domestic and international fashion marketing is the complexity of the business environment. Although the domestic environment is not always sufficiently analysed, most of the environmental factors, such as politics and economics, are fairly well understood by most companies. In the international market, an understanding of the business environment is essential, and an analytical framework is the best way to ensure that none of the important factors are overlooked.

Fashion companies are not only dealing with a business environment that all consumer companies must deal with, but they also make what is essentially a product of cultural significance. Successful marketing operations on an international scale rely on understanding the business and cultural environment, which can be broken down into the following constituent parts:

- Law
- Politics
- Technology
- Social organization
- Aesthetics
- Education
- Values and attitudes
- Religion
- Language
- Economic status

Law and politics

These set the framework within which the international fashion company must operate. If we look at the way in which the EC legislation has impacted on the UK fashion industry, we can note that regulations on issues such as sizing, and VAT on clothing are but examples of how domestic/international legislation affects the industry. Government policy also affects the competitiveness of industries, for example, the Turkish government heavily subsidizes the clothing industry, giving it a price advantage.

The greatest impact on the European fashion industry has been the profound political changes in Central and Eastern Europe, which have led many EC companies to establish production facilities in the region in order to gain cost advantages. Political changes in the Far East attendant on the return of Hong Kong to China will undoubtedly create similar shockwaves in the fashion industry, with the double-edged sword of Western access to the huge Chinese market and at the same time Chinese access to the production and marketing expertise of the Hong Kong fashion industry.

Technology

Technology is an important factor in the fashion marketing strategy. Taken in its broadest sense, it includes both production technology and transportation and communication systems. The decision on whether to export or to invest directly in a country will hinge on many of these factors. Technological improvements have enabled large companies to operate vertically integrated organizations across national boundaries. Technology also plays an important role in international fashion marketing strategy; taking the case of the Russian market, the EIU (1992) survey, *The Clothing and Textile Industry in Eastern Europe*, points out that EC firms have to decide whether to export directly to Russia, with all its attendant problems, or to invest in production technology within countries formerly supplying the USSR and gain access to the market in this way. The third option is the one which has been taken by the UK firm Littlewoods, and this is to invest directly in Russia.

Social organization

By which we mean issues like social class systems, status systems, social mobility and interest groups, which cannot fail to have an impact on fashion marketing. Clothing is used throughout the world as one of the indicators of social class/status and understanding exactly what factors are at work in the country which the fashion company hopes to target can be invaluable. Burberry is a company which has used its understanding of the social organization of the US and Europe to successfully market its products, which are targeted at upper-middle class people in those countries. In Eastern Europe, where the classic men's suit used to be regarded as the uniform of the Communist Party hack, new, Western-style suits are now seen as the uniform of aspiring young businessmen.

Aesthetics

These also determine the success of the fashion marketer's efforts. Understanding what is the target country's idea of beauty, good taste, design and colour can help to develop or modify garments for that market. Evaluating the predominant aesthetic sense of the target market will also ensure that garments are correctly promoted, whether it is in the selection of a fashion model who will wear the garments at a fashion show or the layout and design of promotional literature.

Education

Education affects factors such as the level of skill in the workforce which again will determine whether a large fashion company will choose to invest directly in a country, either by joint venture or direct investment, or whether it will simply export. The highly skilled workforces of Eastern Europe have been an important factor in the decision of many large German and US companies to set up manufacturing units there.

Values and attitudes

These affect not only whether the marketer will decide on direct investment rather than export, but on the way in which fashion will be marketed within a country. Prestige garments, such as Gucci shoes will only appeal to those sections of a society who have positive attitudes to wealth and achievement, such as the US upper-middle classes. The British liberal middle classes, with their uneasy attitude to these factors would need to be targeted in a different way.

   Values and attitudes not only affect the type of products that the fashion marketer will target on any particular customer group, but also the entire marketing approach in the form of the retail outlets selected, the pricing strategy adopted and the promotions used.

Religion

Religion here is taken in its broadest sense to include philosophical systems, beliefs and norms. Taboos and rituals influence not only the styles of fashion that can be marketed to any particular country, but also the best approaches to take with regard to promotional efforts. Apart from the very obvious ways in which religion will affect people's attitudes to fashion, the Moslem's dress code for example, many commentators believe that religion will affect fashion marketing in much broader ways. The frequently noted difference between the flamboyant fashions favoured by the nations such as the Italians and Poles in contrast to the sober fashions favoured by the Germans and Swedes has been attributed to the cultural differences between Catholicism and Protestantism (Curran 1991). It is important not to exaggerate the importance that this cultural factor will have on marketing strategy; after all, Benetton's advertisement featuring a priest and a nun kissing, in defiance of their Church's belief about celibacy for religious orders, was greeted with more criticism in secular England than it was in some of the Catholic countries in continental Europe.

Language

This is one of the most important features that distinguish one culture from another. Although language may be of seemingly little relevance to fashion marketers, it can have far-reaching effects, not only in terms of mass media used for promotions or single communications between buyer and supplier, but with regard to the garments themselves. The choice of language used on labels or on sportswear produced for the mainstream market is a very important factor in the total fashion image. Far Eastern firms favour the use of English language slogans and labels to project an international image; many European firms use Italian language labels and brand names to project a more stylish image.

Economic status

This will also affect the marketing strategy which can be adopted. Economies which are in recession will produce consumers who may regard fashion expenditure as an extravagance, whereas economies which are growing will create an atmosphere in which people are happy to spend more money on fashion items and to adopt different styles more readily.

All the cultural factors which we have discussed, together with the specific business environment in each country (the PESTEL factors outlined earlier) need to be analysed by the fashion marketer in order to decide which new markets to enter or simply to keep abreast of competitors. Global fashion companies, whether in the manufacturing or retailing sectors, are particularly vulnerable to changes both in the profile and expectations of consumers and in the business environments in which they operate (e.g. political change leading to changes in taxation or import policies).

ORGANIZING THE INTERNATIONAL FASHION MARKETING EFFORT

Those companies with a minimal involvement in the international market, the occasional exporters, for example, will make very little effort to plan for the international market. Companies which wish to improve their performance or which already operate in the international market will research the market thoroughly and adapt their marketing accordingly.

Compared to other types of exports, such as machine tools, for example, fashion clothing is uniquely sensitive to the cultural and business environment. Appraisal and selection of countries of operation is of primary importance and this forms the basis of fashion marketing planning at the international level.

The planning sequence for a fashion company wishing to enter international markets is as follows:

- **Establishment of organizational objectives**
- **Appraisal and selection of countries of operation**
- **Appraisal and selection of target market**
- **Development of workable strategies**
- **Implementation**

Establishment of organizational objectives

Before launching into the international market, it is important for the fashion marketer to decide what will be achieved by this move. There are many ways in which we can decide on how to establish our international objectives. For a fashion company, the most important factors will be:

- **Firm's prestige may be enhanced by a global image thus retaining competitive advantage;**
- **Sales volume can be expanded, thereby reducing costs;**
- **Excess production can be sold at times of low demand in home market, and seasonal fluctuations can be levelled out in some firms;**
- **International activities allow the firm to spread its risks;**
- **Competition is international in the fashion industry, international activity is needed to sustain competitiveness.**

Which countries to enter will depend on what the fashion marketer hopes to achieve. For many European companies, expansion in sales volume can only come from international expansion, due to saturated home markets.

Appraisal and selection of countries of operation

No fashion company can hope to penetrate all overseas markets simultaneously, it is therefore important to select those markets which offer the company greatest competitive advantages at the minimum level of risk. The three main areas to research are:

- **Business environment factors**
- **Marketing factors**
- **Financial factors**

The best approach to take is to run a systematic check on these areas, so that the decision to enter a particular market is supported by valid information. The following checklist is a useful aid to decision making.

Checklist for examining the business environment for fashion marketing

Population details
Total population/population growth rate
Income levels, distribution and trends
Geographical concentrations
Educational standards
Language, religious, cultural and social groupings
Consumption trends

Government/political philosophy
Attitude to foreign trade and investment (protectionism is very strong with regard to clothing and textiles)
Taxation policy
Economic planning and control
Attitude towards fashion products (can be very nationalistic)
Attitude towards industrialization (fashion dominated by small- and medium-sized companies)
Foreign exchange policy

Legal/political system
Extent of state intervention in the economy
Political stability
Business law and legislative procedures

Economic resources/system
Existing structure of the economy (agriculture, manufacturing, technology)
Predicted changes in economic structure and rate of exchange
Bankers' actions and attitudes

Standards of living
Cost of labour, capital, materials and equipment
Spread of industrialization
Acceptable currency

Communications
Road systems
Port facilities
Railways
Airports
Telecommunications

Marketing factors checklist
Cost and availability of data
Distribution methods and costs
Competitor garments
Governments regulations on pricing

Financial factors checklist
Government funds for local manufacturers
Taxation systems
Capital availability
Ability to transfer funds

Once these factors have been analysed, the fashion company can then begin to develop and adapt its strategy for the overseas market. Littlewoods has successfully entered the Russian market, but it had to negotiate several problems connected with the fragile economy and the changing economic infrastructure. The biggest problem was that the rouble was not convertible to other currencies. Littlewoods got around this problem by opening two stores, one where customers could buy for 'hard' currency (US$, £, DM, etc.) and another in which customers could purchase using roubles. The profits from the rouble store provide money to cover the costs of running the 'hard currency' store, which in turn provides funds that can be either repatriated or used for buying in garments from overseas suppliers.

Finding accurate data is also a problem when entering new markets. While most EC countries have established market research firms and government data is quite reliable, former Communist countries present a challenge to marketers. Government data is often out of date and production statistics are notoriously unreliable; however, the picture is improving as many large advertising agencies are entering this market and collecting sensitive data that is particularly useful to the fashion marketer.

Appraisal and selection of the target market

Fashion marketing is generally concentrated on two approaches:

- 'mass market' clothes for broad sections of the population
- 'exclusive' clothes for niche markets or elite groups

The choices available to the fashion marketer in deciding how to segment the market and what type of approach to take are many and they are frequently contradictory. While many consumer products, from fast foods to shampoos, have been successfully marketed using the same format in many differing countries, similar formulas which would enable fashion firms to benefit from the economies of scale would be hard to find. Many fashion firms are now concluding that 'international market segments' are a myth and are looking at ways of accessing market segments for fashion on a micro-basis. Indeed, the French government has funded a research project to examine the different consumer characteristics within the EC.

The key factors which determine the shape of the target segments are lifestyle and product benefits. If we look more closely at the shape of international fashion segments, we can see that both the mass market approach, and the exclusive segment approach are applicable at both national and global levels, and that some types of fashion product are more vulnerable to cultural differences than others.

Table 4.1 International marketing matrix

	Mass market	Exclusive market
Global	Undifferentiated branded fashions e.g. jeans	'Classic' styles e.g. Gucci loafers
National	Knitwear and street fashion	Designer fashion

Most fashion companies are small- to medium-sized enterprises and they lack the resources to develop global or even pan-European brands. For companies operating in this sector, the most pressing marketing tasks will be to identify appropriate targets within a given country and to research the consumer profile, taking into account the cultural differences outlined earlier.

Development of objectives

When the business environment of the country/ies has been analysed and the target markets identified, the marketing objectives can be developed in line with the company's overall objectives. At this stage it is important to appraise the company's own resources, management style and marketing mix, and to consider how far any of these will need to be changed or are criteria which will make market entry too difficult, in which case the decision to enter the market may be dropped.

Objectives for a fashion company can be discussed in terms of:

- **Market share**
- **Competitive advantage**
- **Increase in sales**

Objectives can be seen from three major perspectives:

- **Ethnocentric**
- **Polycentric**
- **Geocentric**

These perspectives are discussed below:

- **Ethnocentric** This perspective implies that decisions will be made from a national perspective, the international market will be a secondary factor so that the same marketing programmes will be used in overseas markets. This can result in lost orders: Andrew Hampson's Trading Company dropped a collection by the Italian GE. Pa. Fin group because the Italian firm would not change the product (e.g. sizing and fit) nor the advertising messages to suit a different market.
- **Polycentric** This perspective is based on the view that there are such wide differences between countries and the garments, that the whole marketing programme needs to be adapted to each local environment. The problem for many firms is that the costs of developing separate programmes mean that there are almost no economies of scale.
- Geocentric These marketing perspectives mean that objectives and strategies are based on the understanding that there are similarities *and* differences between national markets. Some adaptation is needed, but there is also scope for standardization. This has been the perspective which has been adopted by Marks and Spencer in their extension into the European market: some ranges have been specially bought or adapted for the French market and other ranges have been made available in both English and French stores.

Development of workable strategies

Once the company has decided what it hopes to achieve in the international market and the perspective that it will adopt, it is then in a position to develop a strategic response. At this stage, the fashion company can decide which marketing mix strategies to adopt to cope with the complexities of the international environment.

Of primary importance is of course the product strategy and the need for changes to the basic garment: the costs of changing production, of using different colours or adding different trimmings, for example. In an international context, branding strategy is also extremely important – the hosiery firm Golden Lady found that style names need to be adapted to suit different markets.

Pricing strategy is inevitably vulnerable to the economic environment; prices set low to achieve market penetration may lead to trade sanctions being imposed, particularly in highly protectionist markets like the US. Pricing will need to be set in line both with product position and with what people in the target market are able to pay. British shoe shops which have opened in Poland have found that it is important to stock some lines which are affordable by a larger market, rather than solely catering for the exclusive segment they initially targeted, as a means of gaining wider market share in the long term.

Distribution strategy will be particularly complex because, even within the EC, distribution channels vary considerably between countries. In other parts of the world, e.g. Africa, distribution channels are frequently centrally planned by government.

In the EC, retailers have immense marketing power and the distribution network is dominated by UK, German and French firms. The power of the retailers means that product specification, pricing and manufacturing terms are often dictated to the producer. Manufacturers are increasingly developing their own retail networks to counteract this effect, as Betty Barclay, Hennes and Episode testify.

Promotion strategy is also subject to national differences, which relate not only to cultural differences between consumers, but also to the power of distribution channels. Companies need to decide whether to promote to the fashion industry as a whole, using shows and PR as the main media, or whether to go for more direct consumer involvement. In France and Italy, there has been an increasing trend to launch new products on both fronts, and to tailor promotional activity to fit both industry and the consumer.

Implementation and control needs to be carefully planned, as for domestic marketing planning. The major difference with international marketing planning is that communications channels need to be fully developed and set out and also clear, identifiable targets need to be established to counteract the difficulties in operating across national borders.

OVERVIEW OF INTERNATIONAL TRADING AREAS SIGNIFICANT TO FASHION MARKETING

The crucial fact about international fashion marketing is that we are dealing with a product that is constantly changing against a backdrop that is also in a constant state of flux. Conditions in the international arena can change almost overnight. However, some broad guidelines can be given as to the conditions which have most impact on the fashion industry.

Europe

Although the single market of the EC increasingly functions as one market, as disparities between tax systems and consumer law, for instance, begin to disappear, cultural differences still prevail. The idea of the Euroconsumer has been the subject of much discussion within the industry, and the consensus is that although some items of clothing can be standardized, successful fashion marketing needs to adapt its approach to different countries.

Outside of the EC, Europe presents itself as sets of potential consumers, for example, Austria, and producers, for example, Turkey. Many manufacturers of clothing, particularly synthetic knitwear at the lower end of the market, have found Turkey to be a fierce competitor, and one which has made significant inroads in the mass market sector.

The former Communist countries present another problem for the fashion marketer. It was once assumed that the countries of the Soviet Union would be a vast market for Western goods, on the basis of superficial indicators like the fact that Soviet citizens were prepared to pay vast sums for Levi's on the black market. The reality is that the USSR's status as a military superpower obscured the poverty and immensely low standards of living of most of the population. Most fashion companies who have chosen to enter this market have done so with long-term objectives in mind and have needed to be extremely flexible. The Russian market is also open to low-priced imports from Turkey and the Far East, which have the advantage of being able to set prices that are within reach for the local market.

The former satellite countries, dominated by the USSR since the partitioning of Europe agreed at Yalta during the Second World War, present a slightly different picture. Hungary and Poland in particular have readily reverted to a free market economy, and many fashion companies have organized successful joint ventures as a means of penetrating these markets. They are also being used as springboards to establish links with other countries in the former USSR whom they previously supplied under the Communist system. Other countries of the former Eastern bloc, such as Romania, do not offer much potential as a market for fashion items at the moment, but they are being examined as potential suppliers or bases for manufacturing.

The future market for the fashion industry in Europe largely depends on the extent to which the EC will develop as a single market and whether it increases its membership. Political stability also plays a major part in assessing the market potential of Europe; after a long period of stability, the continent is entering a turbulent phase and the fashion industry needs to assess the risks carefully.

The Pacific Rim

The countries of the Pacific Rim, e.g. Japan, Taiwan, Hong Kong and the Philippines, have had a significant impact on the fashion industry. Increasingly sophisticated manufacturing technology and willingness to adapt designs has meant that producers from these countries have been able to compete on quality and price in the mass market for some time.

Pacific Rim countries are now beginning to branch out and compete on designs as well, as many Japanese firms are demonstrating. There have also been developments in terms of materials that manufacturers and designers are willing to use, for example, paper, in addition to traditional, natural fabrics like cotton and silk.

North America

Together, the United States and Canada form the largest free trade zone in the world. This effectively gives manufacturers from these countries access to a massive home market, with none of the cultural and language barriers facing international competitors. Additionally, North America has a very protectionist attitude to trade, especially clothing and textiles, resulting in frequent accusations that foreign companies, especially from the Pacific Rim nations are 'dumping' goods at prices below what they cost to produce. Competitor companies from overseas find that US firms are simply not able to keep up with the fashion demands of their customers.

SUMMARY

The fashion industry is vulnerable to changes in the business environment and is widely seen as a manifestation of culture even on a national scale. Therefore, the challenges facing the international fashion marketing manager are profound, because it is the complexity of the marketing environment and the impact of cultural differences that create problems for international marketers.

The key factor in international fashion marketing is to make a thorough and systematic analysis of the country to be targeted before deciding whether to enter the market. The task of selecting which segments to target must be done before marketing objectives are finalized and a strategy for the marketing mix can be developed.

International fashion marketing can take a variety of forms, ranging from small-scale export through to multinational enterprises, and the approach can be either national or global depending on the fashion items being produced and the target market.

DISCUSSION POINTS

1 Taking a checklist for international fashion marketers, carry out an analysis of one country from either Europe or the Pacific Rim area and assess its potential as an export market for a small manufacturer of exclusive knitwear.
2 What changes would need to be made to the marketing mix of a UK hosiery manufacturer wishing to sell in the whole of the EC?
3 How do various cultural factors outlined in this chapter affect the marketing mix of fashion items?
4 Find examples of fashion companies representing the different forms of international business and describe their operations and products.

Chapter 5

The product from its beginnings through to range development

From the fashion marketer's perspective the most complex element of the marketing mix is the product. The fashion marketer needs to ensure that products are constantly updated in line with consumer demand. In this chapter we will examine the creative and marketing process involved in developing products. We will then consider the fashion product life cycle and finally look at ways of developing marketing strategies for the product.

For the purpose of this book we have used three main terms to describe the production of fashion garments:

- **Couture**
- **Ready-to-wear**
- **High street**

It is useful to have an understanding of these and their place in the market before examining the production process.

COUTURE

To become a true couturier is to be bound by the rules laid down in Paris. It was an Englishman named Worth who began the system in Paris, and Paris is still where most couture is produced. The garments are one-offs, it is a way of ensuring quality and originality in the industry; this is monitored by the Chambre Syndicate de la Couture Parisienne.

Available only to the very rich, with dresses costing as much as £60,000, couture collections are supported by other means, as a fashion house could not rely on sales of couture alone. Financial support usually comes from the sales of perfume and cosmetics or from licensing agreements. In France most couturiers are also backed by huge textile companies. The collections appear twice a year to those special clients, buyers and the press.

READY-TO-WEAR

Also known as *prêt-a-porter*, ready-to-wear is produced by the couture houses as an addition to the couture collection, though the prices are still high. Designers also produce ready-to-wear, showing two main collections a year plus mid-seasons. Ready-to-wear has proved very popular and many British designers such as Joseph, Katharine Hamnett and Helen Storey have world-wide success. The collections are usually shown on the catwalk at the shows in London, Paris, Milan and New York. Designers traditionally show in the country where they are based. Some British designers, however, such as Vivienne Westwood and Paul Smith, dissatisfied with the shows in Britain and with a growing awareness of the need to be seen to be European, are showing in Paris and Milan. The young Japanese designers have been using Paris as a base for over a decade.

HIGH STREET

The high street provides a mass market with up-to-date fashion at various prices and caters for many tastes and ages. Dominating the high street in Britain are Sears, Burton and Storehouse, who operate many groups with different types of outlet. Burtons owns the department store Harvey Nichols as well as many chain stores. Each of their chain stores aims for a different section of the market, for example, Top Shop sells to the teenager, Dorothy Perkins to the secretary or young mum.

Other high street names have also carved their own niches: Marks and Spencer has a reputation for affordable quality, Jaeger for quality and style for an older market; The Gap and Jigsaw for fun yet stylish clothes aimed at the young. When or wherever a new shopping development emerges, many of these names will have a store there. The high street usually requires a high turnover of goods and profit and as such the product will usually be made with many variations in order to keep the customer interested.

There are two basic ways of developing new ideas:

- **Product adaptation**
- **Product development**

Sometimes both these methods are used simultaneously to produce a collection.

THE CREATIVE PROCESS

The creation of an idea through to the actual production of a range involves several processes. The mass market works very quickly and is often constrained by tight budgets.

Design is usually completed in-house by the design team. This is headed by the design director/manager and there are usually several designers, a pattern cutter and a sample machinist. Larger organizations may commission smaller companies to design a collection and sample range. This will be worked around a given theme or story, fabric and approximate price.

The image of the design studio filled with glamorous people in perfect surroundings is a myth. New design ideas are not produced out of the blue either; the reality often involves using a combination of many current ideas which are proving popular. If a design sold well last season it may well be reworked, i.e. a different detail added, for this season's collection. As mistakes are expensive, it becomes a difficult and demanding process, often time-consuming and definitely hard work.

TARGET MARKET

The first step involves analysing the consumer, looking at past and present sales figures, evaluating which lines sell well, understanding if the consumer has changed fashion ideas and knowing what will influence the consumer when making a purchase. The recent green movement has meant people, especially the young, have been buying environmentally friendly fabrics.

Once the target market has been decided then the approximate prices for the garments can be arranged. These prices will be finalized much later at the factory, but they will give the design team a budget to work to. Designing the collections is the next stage.

INFLUENCES

All designers must be aware of what other designers are producing. If the firm's budget will allow, then designers will visit the collections at Paris, London, Milan and New York. Designers will try to visit both the couture and the ready-to-wear shows. Trade shows are also important, especially the fabric fairs. As the textile industry works up to two years ahead, it will often be the fabrics that will be most important and influential. All levels of design houses will visit the trade fairs, if they cannot get abroad they will go to London and/or Harrogate.

Fashion prediction consultancies

These consultancies offer a source for ideas and other services for the designer. They can be quite expensive, but most firms realize their value, especially if they cannot afford to send designers to the collections. Companies will also use them in combination with visits to the collections to ensure that they have picked up on the main themes and trends. The fashion prediction consultancy business grew rapidly during the 1980s.

Most consultancies produce their own guides to the coming season. These will include fabric swatches, design interpretations, colourways and textures. Individual fashion companies may employ the consultancy to give a presentation of the following season, consisting of videos, slides and fabric swatches. Examples of such agencies are Promostyl, Nigel French and Design Intelligence.

Magazines

Fashion magazines are essential as they have a great influence on the consumer and it is important that they are kept up to date. In 1989 Bruce Oldfield, employed as a consultant by a Scottish textile firm, was quoted as saying: 'If you really want my advice, don't have November 1987 fashion magazines lying around. That won't keep you in touch.'

The International fashion magazines can be good sources of ideas, not just because of the clothes, but in their layout presentation. Trade magazines such as *Drapers Record, Fashion Weekly* and the American *Women's Wear Daily* are useful for their analysis of trade figures, including best-selling items of the week and predictions of possible best sellers during the season.

Other magazines which are not always categorized as fashion but as style/music magazines can also prove important. As early as 1986 *The Face* magazine produced a feature using sportswear clothing, influenced by the bicycle couriers from New York. For the 1991 Chanel Show, Karl Lagerfield showed cycle shorts as part of his collection.

Other influences

Designers are constantly aware of other media such as television, music, film and art. Pop groups and sports people are particularly copied by young people. When Chelsea Girl produced a black top similar to that Madonna had worn on 'Top of the Pops' they sold out within a week. Paul Gascoigne or 'Gazza', the footballer, uses his famous image and name to sell a brand of tracksuits. Fine artists such as Bridget Riley, Andy Warhol and Van Gogh have had their ideas put onto clothing.

Finally, as up-to-date knowledge of the competition is essential, designers frequently write shop reports. These entail gathering information on styles, variations, colours, sizes and prices from rival retailers. Once in a rival's store, designers can assess what appears to be selling well, what customers are looking at and, most importantly, what they are buying.

PUTTING TOGETHER A RANGE

Once the influence and look has been decided, the range can be drawn up. Designers will produce many sheets of very quick sketches showing variations of a style. From these sketches several designs will be selected and fabrics will be chosen. Sample lengths of fabric will be ordered, most textile manufacturers producing sample lengths of 30 metres. The design assistant and pattern cutter will work together to produce the initial patterns. Once the garment has been cut out, the sample machinist will put it together. The machinist will advise the designer of any problems, for instance, it might be easier to cut it in a slightly different way or the design may not be compatible with mass production.

The designs are then ready for their first showing; this takes place in front of the whole design team. If there are in-house buyers they will also be present. The range can then be finalized in terms of cost, colour and variations of style. Some designs will be rejected because of cost or incompatibility with the range. Manufacture will be discussed and the costs/timescale of production decided.

Design/cuts are rarely perfect first time and the patterns will be recut and made up until they are satisfactory. Occasionally, ranges will never go on show, as such, because they are produced exclusively for one firm. Often these designs are completed up to 12 months in advance as the company realizes it will always sell certain styles, i.e. a classic white blouse.

The final range is then taken to the factory or outworker where a sample is produced. This is usually in one size but some companies demand that the range is produced throughout the sizes. The design company can now see the standard of work; if it is not suitable another producer may have to be chosen. The sample range, known as the sealing sample, will be given either to the buyer or to quality control, so that the standard of the mass-produced items can be checked. The product is now ready to be bought or ordered and the process of mass production can begin. (See the fashion calendar, Figure 7.1, p. 92.)

THE PRODUCT LIFE CYCLE

In general marketing there is a concept known as product life cycle. It is essentially the development and growth of a product on the retail market (for a representation of a fashion product life cycle see Figure A.1 on p. 169). Before the product can begin its life it has to be developed. During this development period, time and money are invested until it is suitable for production. Once ready for production, it can then be introduced onto the market. A product will remain at this stage until a group or groups begin buying the product. As awareness of the product increases, it enters the growth period where the majority of profits are to be made. The product should have the greatest market share and few, if any, competitors at this point. This growth period does not last long and the idea, if it proves popular will be quickly and widely copied, allowing it to enter the maturity stage. At this point the profit margin will begin to decrease, first, as competitors are beginning to take parts of the market share, usually with cheaper imitations, and second, as the item is no longer as fashionable, and finally because new products will be entering the market. The product market will now go into decline. It will either stop being produced or it will find a small but select market for which it will continue to be produced. When a product reaches the maturity stage it is able to extend its life in one of two ways: it can expand the line of products it is presently producing or it can develop a compatible product range.

A good example of extending the product life cycle can be seen in the marketing strategies employed by the manufacturers of the Timberland boot. The Canadian boot was brought to the UK at the beginning of the 1980s. It was sold through select outdoor equipment shops to consumers requiring quality mountain/walking boots. These consumers were the experimenters, trying out a new product, prepared to discard their familiar label. Timberland continued to market itself as the traditionally crafted hand-made Canadian mountain boot. At this point the product began to jump the barrier from serious clothing to a serious fashion item. It began to replace the Doctor Marten shoe. The DM shoe was black, representing an old and sombre mood, it was also becoming too acceptable; copies of the shoe could be found everywhere. The young were looking to new times, they were consumerists having fun and they required new and different party shoes. Youth was enjoying a come-back; they rebelled against the yuppie and Next generation; the 'rave' was born, huge events took place in warehouses or fields. This was no time for neat, delicate shoes – footwear had to be as hard-hitting as the music and the location. Above all it had to be new, and the Timberland fitted the bill. Sales of the boot also benefited from a changing sociopolitical scene. To be green was to be aware; the Timberland had the correct outdoor connotations for a new generation. It was rapidly and extensively copied, not just by shoe manufacturers but also by jean manufacturers such as Levi's and Wrangler. From then on its position as a fashion item was about to go into decline. The original cost of the boot was £110; the high street version cost just £29.99. Timberland began promoting its shoes and other styles of boot to further establish new market positions. At the height of its success the boot could even be bought through mail order catalogues such as Brian Mills.

After the shoes came a range of clothing for men and finally a range of women's clothing. Timberland has changed back to an older, less fickle market. Moreover, it has found a new niche, that is, for quality, stylish, outdoor wear without the twee country look.

The life cycle as a variant of the 'classic' fashion life cycle

The 'classic' product life cycle cannot always be applied to fashion marketing. In fashion marketing the fashion life cycle can be dictated in a number of ways. First, the natural cycle according to the seasons – the weather, particularly in Britain, dictates the purchase of garments, consequently, the consumer will not choose to select summer garments in August. Second, there will be trends which work through certain groups, usually teenagers, and these trends will not have mass appeal nor are they affected by the seasons. Third, a product will move from 'mass market' to 'exclusive market' or vice versa.

The 'bumbag' (small bag worn around the waist) began life as a cycling accessory; as a fashion for mountain biking grew so did the market for accessories and clothing. By 1987 this bag was being worn not just by cyclists but also by nightclub goers, for whom it had become a fashion accessory. Now being produced in a variety of fabrics and colours from cotton tartan to gold PVC, it was the shape that counted. In the spring of 1990 it was beginning to lose its popularity on the street. At this stage couture versions were being produced, Chanel showed a quilted version, Hermès and Gucci brightly coloured bags with the all-important logos on them. Copies of these couture versions were soon available on the high street or market stalls; these gained more kudos because they were fakes – the bag had been born again. Clever retailers spotted that it would be ideal for the person on holiday and the bag is now produced as a travel accessory; as such, it is particularly popular with the 50-plus age group.

The Barbour jacket is another example of a fashion product that had its origins elsewhere. When it was taken on as a fashion item in the 1980s it had country associations and up-market appeal. However, its popularity had been gained in the 1940s and 1950s as an alternative to motorbike leathers. Barbour was able to change the company image back to that of suppliers to officers and gentlemen, a title earned during the First World War. Barbour produced various styles and found a ready market in those 'townies' who wanted to prove that their hearts were really in the country. By the late 1980s, copies of the Barbour sold as 'waxed jackets' were available everywhere from Marks and Spencer to street traders. The prices charged varied, some were even more expensive than the Barbour itself. Even the Australians came on the scene with their version, the Drizabone. The Barbour style was worn by all ages and classes. It briefly became popular for urban youth, especially with the young black market where, worn with a touch of irony, it clashed with high-fashion trainers. As the Barbour now moves into decline as a fashion item, the jacket, with its 1890 origins, can be assured a steady market to traditional country folk.

The life-cycle pattern is essential to the retail of fashion; depending upon the particular target group this can be speeded up regardless of the natural cycle of the seasons.

PRODUCT IDENTITY

In the eyes of the consumer there is no such thing as just a product. A product does not come naked but acquires, due to marketing techniques, a personality or status. The consumer expects to identify and locate a product either by its brand name or label. In the fashion world, the term 'product' can be applied to the type of retail outlet – the shop itself becomes a brand name or label, such as Marks and Spencer or Harrods – providing a 'home' for the fashions. Where the consumer acquires the product becomes itself very much a part of the selling process. Cultivating an identity can result in both brand and store loyalty from the consumer. It is often the label which is more important to the consumer than the quality or suitability of the item.

Among the young, training shoes are a fashionable item. The design is not the main concern, it is the brand name that the consumer seeks. World-wide figures reveal that Nike are the number one sellers with Reebok second; it is these labels that are sought after. Nike and Reebok use famous sports people to endorse their brands which have gained a street credibility. Another brand vying for a top position is L.A. Gear. This company established itself in the 1980s' aerobics boom producing shoes and clothes. It is looking to find favour among the urban youth and used Michael Jackson to promote the brand, with an advertisement not dissimilar to one of the singer's videos. Nike and Reebok are not too concerned; their customers are mainly male and young. Surveys suggest that this consumer does not identify with Michael Jackson. Another image problem is the lack of sufficient sportswear connotations of L.A. Gear; the brand has been sold through Miss Selfridge and the main high street shoe stores. It is therefore unlikely that L.A. Gear will ever gain the kudos that Nike and Reebok enjoy.

While names such as Nike, Reebok and Fila have been able to secure the sports shoe markets, they do miss out because they sell only to sports shops. Their logos are valuable items, in the late 1970s they found themselves being copied and counterfeits were flooding in from the Far East. Today, a youth culture has emerged which involves printing the fashionable logos on all styles of clothing. The logos and designs are reproduced in combination, so a T-shirt may have as many as eight or nine logos on it. The designs are usually limited editions with the screens destroyed so there is no evidence for the Trading Standards Officer. The counterfeiters claim that the multinationals cannot produce adventurous clothing. Retailers who sell the garments claim that they have tried to stock the real labels but, as they are fashion rather than sports shops, they

Plate 5.1 Nike shoe (Air Max Classic)

have been refused. It has also been claimed that the clothes sell because they are 'rip offs'. Logos have become so familiar that they have almost become part of the culture and it could be argued that they have lost their ownership.

The logo or brand name is central to product identity. Creating a product/brand identity does not just involve signs, brochures and business paper, but today includes corporate clothing. The word 'uniform' is avoided, 'career clothing' being the preferred term. Realizing that this is becoming a growing product group, the International Wool Secretariat evolved its Career Clothing Information Bureau (CCIB). The Bureau holds annual awards for the best in career clothing.

Companies are prepared to spend up to £250 per employee in return for quality clothing that has been well designed. The Conran Design Group developed the new BhS house dress in September 1989. Michelle Cappelaese stated:

We wanted a uniform that would last the three to five years we expect an image to be current.

A democratic approach was taken in that staff were offered a number of sample uniforms and asked to give their ideas. Given the number of staff, there were many considerations, such as the range of sizes, ethnic/cultural needs and the need to be adaptable for maternity wear. The conclusion reached by BhS was:

The design was excellent, because it was the kind of design that would work across the full age range, which was vitally important for us.

The fabric chosen for corporate clothing has also undergone many changes. Often produced in nylon or polyester, corporations stated that this made them easier to clean, but it did not consider staff comfort. The use of poly/cottons, wool mixes and even some 100 per cent natural fibres creates a smarter look. It also has the effect of garments becoming more like the staff's personal wardrobe. The supplying of staff with garments has become a very involved process. However, it has been stated that:

It can be a highly effective marketing tool when it forms an integral part of the corporate image.

PRODUCT MARKET STRATEGY

Given that all products have a finite 'shelf' life and therefore new products/markets will have to be developed, it is important to understand the various methods that can be employed.

According to Ansoff (1988) it is essential to find the 'common thread', that is, the relationship between present and future directions of the firm. A company could be described either by product-line characteristics or by customer type. If it is the product that is important then the distribution becomes the common thread as there may be a wide range of different users. The consumers' needs could also describe the company. In order to find the common thread, the product market scope can prove useful. According to Ansoff (1988) this 'specifies the particular industries to which the firm confines its market position'.

There are four key points to be addressed:

1 **What markets should be served?**
2 **What form should the product take?**
3 **What should the product do for the user?**
4 **For whom is the product most important?**

We expand upon these key points opposite:

1 This involves realizing and identifying customer needs. In fashion/ clothing this means identifying the customer's needs in terms of age, price range and lifestyle requirements. For example, Top Shop (part of the Burton group) serves the teenage to 25-year-old market. The clothes are mainly for socializing rather than career wear. This audience requires fashion garments and will 'buy something different for Saturday night'. Consequently, a low price with a high-fashion look rather than a quality garment is required.

2 The form of the product will in this case be the wide range of low-priced garments. This also means that Top Shop will need to have a high stock turnover, constantly introducing new styles to keep its audience interested.

3 This is allowing the users access to a high-fashion look that is within the consumers' price range. Enabling a different look to be achieved, maybe for some on a weekly basis.

4 For whom is the product most important? In the case of Top Shop, as the fashions quickly become redundant, there is no prestige value for the company. The product is important in terms of its high turnover and therefore quick cash recovery. The development of the product package makes it important in terms of where Top Shop fits in within the Burton group.

Developing where the common thread lies can provide a basis for the development of new products or new markets.

It is useful to observe Ansoff's Product Market Matrix. This works in four ways, depending on product and customer needs. In some cases only one of the marketing strategies may be used. In the case of Hornes menswear all four strategies have been employed. The group aims to provide quality clothing to the older ABC1 market. Hornes and its younger-image chain Zy were taken over by the Sears group in mid-1987. Sears was able to acquire 42 Hornes shops and 11 Zy outlets, a suit factory, Hornes Corporate Clothing Company and the marketing firm Worth Valley, which has the Pierre Cardin menswear, making them the main UK licensee. As Hornes also had a credit card, Hornes Executive Club, Sears gained another 35,000 account holders to its own corporate card.

The four ways in which the product market can work are given below:

Market penetration

If there is an existing customer need and an existing product then the market share needs to be increased. This involves designing market strategies in order to reduce competition. To increase customer awareness of the product several strategies can be employed: price reduction, promotional techniques, advertising, internal and external expansion.

Hornes decided to expand, increasing its own outlets from 42 to 60 and the Zy outlets from 11 to 40. Moving away from the southeast base, they opened in the north of England and Scotland, and backed up this strategy with regular advertising and promotion to attract new custom and retain original customers.

Product development

An existing customer need can be attracted to a new product. This could involve the extension of existing lines or the development of new ranges. Using Hornes' strong identity, they created own brands and explored the concept of a shop within a shop. Hornes mixed casual wear with quality tailored wear, introducing ranges such as Walker and Shaw, a collection for the more mature customer, Northpoint, a refined leisure/casual wear range and Hornes Club, executive/business wear with an emphasis on quality. Product development ensures customer interest and while some customers may buy across ranges others will identify with one brand.

Market development

When a product exists, market development ensures new customers. Finding new customers can involve mass advertising and promotion, which can be costly. The Sears take-over, while giving Hornes' customers who owned cards access to other Sears groups, also allowed Hornes access to the other 400,000 Sears cardholders. Hornes used this information to begin a direct mailing programme. The group has also considered mail order, which could prove attractive to new customers.

Diversification

Diversification happens when both a new product and new customers are sought. Diversification can mean a move into something totally unrelated to the original product, although usually, in order to maintain corporate identity, diversification is within the same product type.

There are basically four types of diversification:

- **Horizontal**
- **Vertical**
- **Lateral**
- **By licence**

- **Horizontal**   Diversification of this type involves the addition of new products which are related to the old product line and is probably the most common method of diversification. Hornes had already diversified through its additional Zy shops. When the company became part of the Sears group there were some attractive benefits. The British Shoe Corporation (part of the Sears group) could supply Hornes, enabling them to provide accessories as well as clothing. Further, they were able to use Dormie, the formal-wear hire concession. Using these two products, Hornes was becoming a complete store. Managing director Stuart Rowland was quoted as saying: 'Men are generally regarded as lazy shoppers . . . they rarely go into shops, especially clothes shops, and when they do we want to sell them all the clothes in one go.' Horizontal diversification offers the lowest risk and requires the least effort. Its main advantage is that the original product has an audience, a distribution network and established outlets. There is also an identity and image which the clientele recognizes.

- **Vertical** Vertical diversification happens when raw materials purchased for one product are integrated into the product mix. Through its expansion into different ranges, Hornes was able to use suppliers and fabrics both for its own brands and the own brands of Zy, thus enabling greater economies of scale. The acquisition of the suit factory meant both stores could be supplied, strengthening its own market position. Owning the factory also meant that they had greater control of the overall quality of the products.
- **Lateral** In this case diversification involves the return on a company's investment of either a new company or product. In the case of the Sears buyout, Hornes employed dynamic managers who were able to strengthen the acquired firm.
- **By licence** This approach to diversification means that the company buys the rights of a famous name or brand. This allows the manufacture and retail of goods under the brand name. Using the Pierre Cardin label to produce goods, Hornes is able to have access to a prestigious range.

PRODUCT DIFFERENTIATION

The theories presented by Knee and Walters (1985) suggest that this can happen in two ways:

First, the brand attempts to change the attitude of its customers towards it.

The British womenswear middle market has since 1986/7 undergone a facelift. Before this period the British companies in this market had been out of step with both the up-market designer labels and the cheap and cheerful young chain store fashions.

German companies such as Mondi, Laurel, and Escada were able to capture the market for 25–45-year-old, middle-income women. Adopting a youthful approach, they were completely successful and had no competition from the home market. British companies such as Windsmoor, Mansfield, Aquascutum and Jaegar had a reputation for quality, but fashion- or design-conscious they were not. The problem, which they either had not realized or not addressed, was that women in their thirties/forties no longer submitted to traditional middle-aged attitudes. Today's woman, encouraged by the glamorous and well dressed such as Princess Michael of Kent, Joan Collins and Stephanie Beecham, wants to look young. Although this woman may be married or have children, she is not going to give up work or fashion.

The solution the British companies soon discovered was to invest in the use of top advertising agencies. These agencies hired top models and photographers and produced *Vogue*-like fashion images. Jaegar found that it was having to undergo another image change. The company had been established in 1884 manufacturing Dr Gustau Jaegar's Sanitary Woollen System Underwear, products endorsed by both Oscar Wilde and George Bernard Shaw. During the Second World War, Jaegar became a label associated with good-quality utility wear. Frequently having designs featured by *Vogue*, the garments were also endorsed by the government as suitably frugal. The company continued to build a clientele, selling mainly through boutiques and small shops in the UK. However, its new high-fashion image was often incompatible with the reality of these retailers. Jaegar found their goods were being sold alongside other makes whose design and price were quite different. In 1987 the company took the step of selling through its own outlets, retaining only concessions within department stores. Jaegar completely refurbished its own stores in a modern, bright and clean black and white style which reflected the advertising that portrayed a busy glamorous urban woman in modern clothing that retained a quality and sophistication. Although the Jaegar advertising showed the woman in a short skirt, that length was not actually obtainable in their shops.

The British woman responded extremely well to these changes, and while the product had not changed that much, it managed to lose the frumpy associations and gain a positive image and attitude from its clientele.

Second, the brand can present itself to the consumer as offering something different from its competitors.

The jeans market is extremely competitive, especially when jeans themselves are no longer considered fashionable. During the beginning of the 1980s Levi's found themselves in a difficult position. They were unable to gain a foothold in the then current designer jeans market. Levi's had also diversified, producing other types of clothing including suits. The company was lost and it seemed a rather anonymous label.

Taking stock, Levi's decided to go back to what the company had originally started producing – the 501 jean. Enlisting the help of a top advertising company, they sought nostalgic images that appealed to the young. James Dean and Marlon Brando proved to be renowned for their patronage of the 501. The most important aspect of these film stars was that they were glamorous, decadent, running on the wild side of life. They had a sex appeal that had youth appeal. Using model Nick Kamen, with a soundtrack of Marvyn Gaye's 'I Heard it Through the Grapevine', the advertisment, set in a 1950s launderette, was immensely popular. The advertisement was not selling jeans but rather a design classic. Continuing with the idea of Levis jeans as a sought-after commodity, their other brands sold well. In 1990 the company produced an advertisement very cleverly calculated to take the product into the 1990s. At this stage many of their competitors were producing similar 1950s-style advertisements. Levi's showed a man riding up the lift on a Harley Davidson (the music was Steve Miller's 'The Joker'); there are mock gasps as he rides across the stockbroker's floor. Stopping at a terminal, he presents a female broker with a pair of Levis, she lets down her hair and removes her city suit replacing it with 501s. To the cheers of the other traders, they ride away down the lift and out of New York (or into another era?). In advertising terms it was rather like having the last word.

Pepe, another jeans manufacturer, found in market research tests that advertisements having an obvious sex appeal were associated with Levi's. Breaking the ground-rules in their advertisement, there was no music, no nostalgia and no story. It merely depicted a group of people sitting in a park, giggling and laughing. The screen went blank leaving only the Pepe logo and slogan 'Live today as though it's your last'.

The product, while maintaining a consistent image has to be seen to be changing, which is not always possible with the design. Levi's produced the 501s in original denim, then stone-washed, white and black and finally coloured jeans. This kind of approach enables the life cycle of the product to be extended yet allows the particulars of the advertising to remain constant. Fashion products have to be marketed in this way while manufacturing must always reflect an awareness of the changing seasons and the occurrence of fads.

SUMMARY

In this chapter we have examined what is meant by the term 'product' and have also considered the product development process as it specifically relates to the fashion industry.

We have examined concepts which assist us in understanding our product and its performance in the market-place, the fashion life cycle, product identity and brand personality. We have also examined marketing strategies for products, in particular product differentiation.

To conclude, the emphasis must be on awareness; the consumer is always changing and it is essential that a company understands and adapts – new products and services must continually be sought. These are the most common methods used:

- Develop internally
- Develop with a product development agency
- Obtaining a licence from another company
- Joint venture
- The acquisition of an existing producer

By using managers, employees, customers or development agencies, ideas for these new companies can be found. The new product strategies may include:

- Modification of existing products
- Addition of complementary products
- Entry into an existing market which is new to the company
- Development of a new market through the introduction of a new product

DISCUSSION POINTS

1 Choose a fashion item that is very popular at the moment and trace its origins, examining its development in terms of its life cycle. What would you do to ensure its survival?
2 Take a mass-appeal product with a recognizable name, examine how it has established itself as different from its competitors. Try to understand how this differentiation process has taken place.
3 The jeans market is huge, select three different brands of jeans and examine their various personalities and identities.
4 Your company is trying to decide whether store staff should wear their own clothes or a uniform or a selection of the stock. The shop sells to the female 18–25 market, but the all-female staff are aged from 16–30. Which policy would you decide upon and why?

Chapter 6

Place in the fashion marketing mix

'Place' is the term used by fashion marketers to cover the means by which garments become available to consumers. The whole issue is complex and is crucial to the success of the marketing effort. In this chapter we will focus on three areas of prime importance:

- Location
- Operations – logistics, warehousing and transportation
- Channels of distribution and retailing

LOCATION

Location of manufacturing capacity is becoming less important as technology and transport improve. Thus The Gap is able to manufacture in the Far East and distribute in Europe and America.

For the fashion retailer, however, location is of prime importance, both in terms of positioning the store and in reaching the target market. Niche shops such as Knickerbox and Tie Rack, for example, realized the advantages of establishing themselves in railway stations where purchases would be made quickly and turnover could be high.

OPERATIONS – LOGISTICS, WAREHOUSING AND TRANSPORTATION

The producers

The organization of the manufacture of garments in the fast-moving fashion industry needs to be understood by marketers if they are to meet the consumer. Usually, only the larger retail concerns have their own design and manufacturing bases. This means they can bypass the wholesaler, can direct supply and have full control of product specification. These manufacturers will be producing goods either for other people or under their own label.

It is quite common for designers or companies to use a type of factory known in the trade as 'outdoor'. Outdoor workers range in size from fully equipped small workplaces to machinists working from home. They are often used by smaller concerns or designers who cannot afford full-time production. One of the main concerns for designers using outdoor workers is that of trust. Outdoor workers often have access to the designer's latest creations, fabrics and labels.

It is common for unscrupulous workers to use fabric leftovers to produce 'cabbage'. 'Cabbage' is the term used to describe the garments made without the designer's knowledge and obviously sold through another outlet. Some examples of 'cabbaging' have included instances of designer labels being used. Designers often split work between several outdoor workers depending on specializations.

The warehouse

Most large concerns, whether manufacturers, retailers or both, have their own warehouse. This is the place where goods can be subject to quality control (if this has not been done at the factory), repackaged if necessary, priced and ticketed, allocated and finally packed for leaving the warehouse.

The layout of a warehouse is important and automation is becoming increasingly essential as the manufacturer of fashion goods will have a deadline from the buyer and will be under contract to deliver goods by that date. Many goods will have to be priced, a process often known as 'kimballing'. This is named after the small machine, which operates like a gun, that attaches the price ticket to the garment through the label with a small piece of plastic. This is done manually but usually reasonably quickly and any repackaging, such as putting together packs of underwear for different retailers, can also be carried out at this stage. The goods will then be ready for allocation. The information carried on the ticket can be used for stock-monitoring purposes.

Allocation

This process has to be carried out carefully for many problems can arise. First, retailers will require a comprehensive range so that goods can be put on sale the moment they arrive. It is the responsibility of the allocator to make sure that there are an equal number of skirts/trousers to go with jumpers/shirts or blouses. The sizes must also co-ordinate; it is no use sending size 16 tops to go with size 8 bottoms! The colours must also match, and there may be as many as eight different colourways. The main concern for the allocator is that the manufacturers will often be producing one type of garment, i.e. skirts until the factory changes production. If the warehouse is being supplied by a number of manufacturers then the situation can become quite chaotic. Finally, individual retailers like to believe that they are the only customer. Small boutiques in particular do not like to see their competition, often department stores, obtaining stock before them. The allocator's job can be likened to that of a diplomat. Even where the manufacturer and retailer are the same, competition across the area branches is often fierce.

The allocator usually works with a computer, which holds the following information: the amount and type of stock in the warehouse, and the stock already received by retailers including dates, production schedules and the retailers' accounts. Some firms still operate files manually but this can be time-consuming and mistakes, such as sending out goods to retailers with debts outstanding, can be made.

Once the allocation is made goods are packed and labelled in order that they can be moved as quickly as possible. This is for everyone's benefit; space in the warehouse is always at a premium, the goods will not be paid for until they arrive at the store and retailers require stock as soon as possible.

Delivery and transportation

Most manufacturers operate a 'just-in-time' delivery service, whereby goods are delivered to the store ready to put on display (i.e., ticketed, packaged, on hangers). This form of delivery is becoming more popular due to the use of computer technology in production and distribution. A just-in-time system offers cost cuts in storage and manufacture. Delivery is not always straightforward, for instance, the seamen's strike of 1988 meant that many clothing stores' summer stock was stuck on the wrong side of the channel.

Transportation from the warehouse can be done using a variety of methods; the company may have their own delivery vans or if it is a very small concern the reailer may have to collect. Larger companies will use the services of groups such as Tibbett and Britten. The vans are equipped with rails so goods can be moved automatically from the warehouse to the van with no manual assistance. For smaller parcels many firms find it cost-effective to use the Post Office, particularly if goods are going abroad.

STOCK CONTROL

This is one of the key factors in distribution and retail. The aim of stock control is to keep an optimum stock level in the retail outlet. If there is too little stock then the amount of sales volume is restricted. This limits the potential for greater profits as the gross margin will be restricted, customers will notice lack of choice in both size and style and this could lead to them going elsewhere. Too much stock means the retailer is paying for unsold stock. The interest charged on stock investment will result in lower gross and net margins, and to clear the stock it may be necessary to further lower gross margins by reducing prices. In order to control stock three main systems are in use:

- **Unit**
- **Financial**
- **Combination**

- **Unit stock control** By this method the units sold are counted; because of this it is a method suitable for fashion goods. Stock is physically counted and often divided into merchandise sub-groups which helps with model stock planning. Disadvantages with the system are that it does not control profit and therefore requires a back-up monitoring system. It also requires that the market is continually monitored to observe trends in buyer behaviour.
- **Financial stock control** This method uses the amount of cash available to monitor stock, and such a system can be used by itself or in conjunction with unit stock control (in which case it is known as combination control). Financial stock control compares the total value of stock with the value of sales it has produced. It has two main advantages: it is cheap to operate as retailers are comparing cash-till figures with stock investment and it also allows regulation of the gross margin. For these reasons it is the most common method of stock control.
- **Combination stock control** This simply means that both the above methods are used in conjunction.

Periodic and perpetual stock control

Periodic stock control will take place at specified times of the year such as the end of the season. Three main methods are used:

- **Stocktaking**
- **Stock check**
- **Stock calculation**

- **Stocktaking** This can be the most effective and comprehensive method of the three as every item is counted and valued. Merchandise is sub-divided into categories, lines, then style, colour and price. The age of goods is considered to calculate depreciation and a current valuation can then be given. This produces figures which can then be used for final accounts, determining shrinkage, true gross margin and stock-turn rates; it also helps staff get to know the merchandise.
  Stocktaking does, however, involve massive preparation. Layout

plans have to be prepared, sorting categories determined. Goods have to be checked for lost tickets, those goods not on sale, i.e. at the PR company or on window display, must also be included. It can be an expensive exercise, and initially all staff have to be fully briefed. The retailer must then decide whether to close the outlet during a normal trading day or pay staff overtime for working a Sunday or evenings. Staff usually find stocktaking boring and tedious because it is so extensive.

- **Stock check** A simplified version of stocktaking, this method assesses the selling rather than the value. A stock check will often just be concerned with the quantities, price lines and assortment, e.g. size, style, colour, etc.
- **Stock calculation** This method involves taking the last stocktaking value and either adding deliveries or subtracting sales during the period. It gives an approximate value of the stock, although obviously does not take into consideration shrinkage or depreciation.

Perpetual stock systems continually monitor deliveries and sales. Although this approach can prove costly if done by hand, using computers it has become cost effective. EPOS or electronic point of sale was the first computer system to be used in this way. It has great advantages for the retailer; immediately goods have been sold the sales can be calculated and studied, and trends can be found on a day-to-day basis.

The system can be set up to include purchase returns, part-exchanges, replacements, stock written off and depreciation, thereby ensuring accurate financial and unit control. The computer can also be programmed to phone through replacement orders to a central ware-house every evening for next-day delivery. An advancement of EPOS has been EDI or electronic data interchange system which allows still further possibilities. It is essentially an electronic postal service which delivers information from one company's computer to another. This cuts down the need for paperwork and speeds up retailer–supplier links as invoices and general information can be produced by the computer. Marks and Spencer has developed a system whereby even their small suppliers can be part of the network.

The main advantage appears to be the lack of risk involved, especially for fashion retailers. If, early on in the season, certain lines are not selling, then the manufacture of those items can be cancelled. This prevents unpopular merchandise taking up shelf or stock space as the manufacturer also receives descriptions of fast-selling lines.

In order for there to be successful marketing communication between manufacturers and retailers, especially where manufacturers supply only one retailer, the use of this system appears to be essential.

With distribution there are always stock shortages, often termed 'shrinkage or leakage'. There are two kinds:

- **Physical**
- **Clerical**

Physical shortage can happen to the business for the following reasons:

- **Theft**   both external, by members of the public, or internal, by the staff. One method of stealing is known as 'sweethearting' where goods are sold to friends of the staff at less than the retail price.
- **Spoilage**   occurs when goods displayed are damaged, for example, by dust or sunlight if in the window. Careless customers can tear or leave make-up on goods when trying them on.
- **Loss**   may occur if goods on loan to PR companies or for fashion shoots are not returned.
- **Over-issue**   means that, for example, when packing small items carelessness leads to too many items being included in one pack. A lucky find for the customer perhaps, but not so for the retailer.
- **Under-supply**   is caused by incorrect counting when goods are delivered – this could result in fewer goods accepted than have been paid for.

Clerical shortages can also happen in a number of ways; namely through errors in physical stocktaking, book-stock calculations or totaling of stock sheets.

CHANNELS OF DISTRIBUTION AND RETAIL

Once the product has been ordered and manufactured it has then to reach the appropriate store and consumer. The retail environment is constantly undergoing developments to match the effects of economic and consumer changes. The high street has suffered in recent years; the effect of high interest rates has been that shoppers are having to find more money to keep up mortgage repayments thereby reducing their disposable income. Consumers have also been less keen to use credit cards. The stores themselves have also suffered from the rise in inflation and the introduction of the uniform business rate, resulting in many businesses closing. Only those who have owned much of their own floor space have survived. There have been conflicting reports which suggest that, although the number of high street stores is falling, the overall number of shops is increasing. This could reflect the number of out-of-town or fringe developments that are now proving popular, such as the Cornhill Shopping Centre in Darlington. With these new developments comes the opportunity for a growing variety in individual stores and with this in

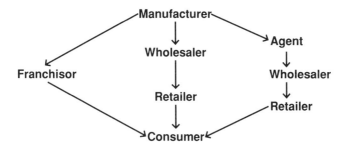

Figure 6.1 The channels of distribution

mind many department stores have been redeveloped as unit shop schemes, such as Whiteleys of Bayswater and the Co-op, Birmingham.

Many different channels of distribution exist for getting the product to the consumer, as can be seen in Figure 6.1. The channel of distribution can be complex, but some manufacturers sell direct to customers. Usually these are smaller manufacturers such as Clothkits and, indeed, Laura Ashley began in this way.

The wholesaler

The wholesalers (or middlemen) who distribute the garments may also be the manufacturers of the garments, but not always the retailers. Companies such as Jonathon Miller and Jeffrey Rogers both manufacture and sell wholesale their own label. Wholesalers are useful for the retailer, they 'break bulk', in other words they sell in smaller quantities often with a minimum order value, e.g. £300. Permanent stockholders often operate a cash-and-carry service so goods can be acquired immediately. Some fashion wholesalers will have a showroom and employ models so garments can be viewed being worn. Also operating as wholesalers are:

- **Importers** These wholesalers reduce the expense of research, communication and buying trips. They often offer specialist merchandise, e.g. Thai silks.
- **Agents**   They do not hold stock, only samples, but will often travel to retailers as well as having a permanent showroom. Agents will often handle several different 'names' and types of goods. They provide manufacturers with a cost-effective means of selling and the retailer (usually small business) with opportunities to buy.

Retailers

There are various forms of retail organization, some of which will retail in several ways. For example, Miss Selfridge has its own stores, operates concessions and offers mail order through Freemans catalogues. The main types of retail organizations are:

- **Department stores**   John Lewis, House of Fraser
- **Supermarkets/hypermarkets**   Tesco, Asda
- **Variety chain stores**   Marks and Spencer, BhS
- **Multiple chain stores**   Next, Top Shop, Hornes
- **Co-operatives**   Shopping Giant
- **Franchises**   Benetton, Stefanel
- **Discounts**   What Everyone Wants, Mark One
- **Independents**   Whistles, Pollyanna, Sunday Best, Jenners
- **Mail order**   Gratton, Brian Mills, Kingshill
- **Markets**   Camden Lock, Trade Hall

Department stores

Department stores have tried to regain popularity having suffered as the multiple stores have expanded. They have also lost customers to the out-of-town developments as customers are showing a preference for shopping away from the town centre because such developments offer easy access and parking and a wide variety of stores to choose from. Department stores are able to use the space available to operate the 'shop-within-a-shop' concept known as a concession. The wide use of concessions enables a range of tastes to be catered for. This can have a detrimental effect, making the store appear almost like a bazaar. Space management should be carefully considered. With a large amount of different merchandise, the store's image and operating policy should be distinct. This will help the consumer recognize the store rather than the concession. John Lewis states that 'the customer is never knowingly undersold', they also give special customer services such as free alterations of garments.

Supermarkets/hypermarkets

Supermarkets have never been known in the UK for their retail of fashionable clothing, however, over the past few years this has begun to change. Tesco has extended their clothing range to include womens- and menswear. Within the womenswear and menswear ranges they offer both formal and casual clothing which is produced exclusively for Tesco. As part of their buying policy they include underwear from well-known manufacturers such as Jockey and Gossard.

Buying fashion from supermarkets is not new on the Continent, in fact in France it is where most people purchase their clothing. Groups such as Monoprix have a reputation for retailing fashionable, quality goods at affordable prices. The single market will inevitably mean that some European companies will try to establish supermarkets in the UK and, in the longer term, UK customers will become more accustomed to purchasing fashion at the supermarket.

Variety chains

The variety chain store is so-called because it offers a variety of goods, i.e. shoes, womenswear, children's clothing, etc. Variety chain stores have continued to attract customers – the well established, Marks and Spencer and BhS have kept their reputations for value for money. Customers have remained loyal to the traditional brand names, finding that they now offer the same level of choice as the multiple stores. The main reason for their survival is that they can be adaptable in their choice of merchandise. Marks and Spencer found during a period of high interest rates that customers were reluctant to spend large amounts on clothes, but they would, however, treat themselves to cosmetics and toiletries. As long as customer behaviour is carefully observed, this adaptability can ensure the variety chain stores growth in periods of economic uncertainty.

Multiple

The multiple chain store offers one type of clothing, such as womenswear or menswear, usually within one price range to a defined customer. It is the most common type of store on the high street. The consumer has become dissatisfied with the image and merchandise of many of these stores, particularly as the late 1980s saw many Next-style copies.

Multiples have begun to investigate the possibilities of catering to regional tastes. With large buying powers, financial resources and prime sites, the multiple is well served to cater to consumers' changing tastes. Market research can reveal customer preferences to facilitate this, but the retailer must also examine other factors such as the future of the economic climate, the property market and demographic changes. These factors will provide clues for offering the ideal price, product and environment to the customer. It is estimated that the multiples have approximately 70 per cent of the market share. The 1990s offer both opportunities and pitfalls for the multiple as the consumer seeks a more individual image.

Co-operatives

The co-operative was formally established in Rochdale in 1884. The basis of the idea was simple: people put money into the enterprise and were entitled to dividend on the profits. Co-operatives are extremely popular in the Third World, where they offer those with few resources the opportunity to invest and to gain from this investment. In the UK they are not known for their retail of fashion, but they do provide value-for-money basics.

Franchising

Franchising as a method of retailing fashion has been a concept slow to catch on in Britain. A franchise is operated by an individual (franchisee) who 'owns' a property and sells for a small fee or royalty the producer's (franchisor's) products. The franchisee will use the name, image and know-how of the franchisor. The most famous franchises in Britain are Benetton, The Body Shop and Tie Rack. Franchising is, however, set to increase, with the value of franchising in the UK estimated at £9.86 million, in 1993.

There are advantages for the franchisee: all the advertising is undertaken nationally, the name is usually well known and the company has a ready niche in the market. The franchisor is able to distribute goods nationally without the expense of operating retail outlets, which are usually on prime sites. Many British producers are beginning to consider such operations. Coppernob began its franchise venture only a few years ago and has found it to be very successful. To prevent inexperienced franchisees, who lack knowledge about the fashion industry, from making mistakes, Coppernob organizes all merchandise. In other words, they choose the merchandise the franchisee will sell and they also organize the stock flow. French and Italian franchisors have great experience and are keen to enter the UK which they view as a valuable market. Stefanel, an Italian company estimates that they will have 70 UK franchises in operation by the mid-1990s. They have a different approach to Coppernob and believe that the franchisee should have a choice of stock as this will help cater for regional variations. Stefanel will help the franchisee by providing fashion trend information, a computer accounting package and presentations on merchandizing as well as the shop design.

As a method of retailing, franchising is ideal for rapid expansion. Given present consumer requests for individualism, franchisors will have to consider giving the franchisee more freedom. It is also interesting to note that other well-established firms such as Joseph Tricot are entering into franchise arrangements.

Independents

The independent store has recently gained much ground in the high street. The consumer has been attracted by more individual choice and a high level of personal service. In 1989 independents overtook the multiples, with turnover up by 9 per cent. The problem for independents is that they are vulnerable to sudden changes in the local economy. For example, Pollyanna, based in Yorkshire, only just survived the miners' strike in the early 1980s. Some independents such as Whistles (London, Oxford, Glasgow) have large buying powers with the ability to control the quality of goods and services. It is these smaller independent chains that could offer serious competition to the multiples.

Discounts

The discount store is not a type as such (it can be independent or multiple) but it is a phenomenon that has grown in popularity in the UK in recent years gaining 12 per cent growth due to the economic climate. Approximately 15 per cent of clothing is retailed using discounts, through discount chains, 'low lead-in' offers and market stalls. Stock comes from a variety of sources, usually overseas where labour and production costs are low, i.e. in such countries as Korea, India, Taiwan and Greece, and also includes end-of-season merchandise from high street retailers and current stock which manufacturers/wholesalers have been unable to sell. The famous discount names on the high street are What Everyone Wants, Ethel Austin and Mark One.

Mail order

During the 1980s mail order was given a new lease of life. Although it had existed previously, it was very much aimed at those people who could not afford to buy clothes in one full payment, so it offered weekly credit terms. The clothes that were promoted were often of low quality and were not usually considered fashion items. The presentation of the clothes was often considered to be down market and delivery was notoriously slow.

Things began to change when George Davies launched his Next Directory, a catalogue which not only offered quality garments but was itself beautifully presented, with swatches of fabric so customers knew exactly what they were buying. Next offered 48-hour delivery on goods and the only credit offered was via their own card. Next did run into problems with delivery and the company had not calculated for the number of returned garments. However, a new standard for mail order had been established.

Those existing catalogue companies benefited from the de-stigmatizing of the catalogue and took the opportunity to upgrade their services. Many of them enlisted the services of named designers, used well-known models and offered a 48-hour delivery service. Catalogues also benefited from the recession, with many new customers taking the option of buying on credit.

The catalogue has developed, the launch of the more upmarket Kingshill, which retails the designs of designers such as Paul Costelloe, Caroline Charles and Margaret Howell, and the fact that many retailers are now offering a delivery service means that mail order has become a viable outlet.

The Magalogue

This is a new venture for George Davies and was initially launched through the Daily Express. The idea behind it was that the magazine would be sold on a monthly basis with customers ordering from each issue. There were no credit terms offered but the goods were very reasonably priced. This concept developed and has been relaunched as Xtend. Offering fashionable goods at reasonable prices Xtend now competes with other magalogues such as Racing Green.

Markets

The market has been a traditional outlet for retailing textiles and fashion over many centuries. For the most part, markets offer the chance for retailers to begin their business with low overheads and little stock required. On the whole they are places where people can buy cheap clothing, which has often been rejected by other retailers, termed 'seconds'.

The market has, however, become popular, and there are many fashionable markets such as Camden Lock in London and The Trade Hall in Halifax where more exclusive goods can be found. Many young designers find these markets attractive places to start their businesses; John Richmond and Helen Storey began in this way.

SPACE MANAGEMENT AND STORE PRESENTATION

The number of retailers in the 1980s increased dramatically creating a large amount of retail selling space. Unfortunately, the number of consumers has not increased, leading to massive competition.

Retailers have concentrated their efforts on the planning and design of stores to entice the customer. According to Witin Sanghavi (1987) two main objectives of retail space management should be identified:

1 Increase productivity of the selling space through better utilization of the space;
2 Optimum allocation of available space to departments to achieve budgeted market share.

There are four categories for the allocation of floor space:

- **Selling space**
- **Merchandise space**
- **Customer space**
- **Store personnel space**

The amount of selling space should be carefully calculated. It will influence the location of goods, space for customer movement and the positioning of counters, cash tills and staff. To allocate for merchandise space the product type should be identified:

- **Main selling space**
- **Secondary sales**
- **Goods relating (add-on sales)**
- **Spontaneous purchases**

Space can then be allocated in proportion to the contribution such goods will make to the sales and profit. Often referred to as the sales-productivity-ratio method, this approach takes into account percentage turnover, percentage of profit and percentage of space based on past records.

The retailer should access space carefully and not calculate too simplistically. For instance, if women's lingerie occupied 7 per cent of the total floor space and the store gained 11 per cent of its total sales from that department, then the retailer may consider expanding the department to 11 per cent in line with sales. This may not, however, increase lingerie sales, total sales of 11 per cent could be the optimum amount possible given the store's clientele.

The use of a model stock plan as a guide to space allocation of products is another method. Retailers should use their own records, look at competitors' planning and decide minimum footage requirements per product range.

The customer space should then be examined as this will affect the overall layout. There are generally two types of customer:

- **Those who wish to make a purchase, planned buys;**
- **Those who wish to browse but could make an impulse purchase**

Customers should be used as a source of information for space allocation, since they will be reluctant to buy unless their needs are met. For the first type of customer the following list of questions provides a guideline for market research:

- **Are the goods easily seen?**
- **Are similar goods placed nearby?**
- **Are prices clearly marked (especially for the price-sensitive customer)?**
- **Is information available?**

- Is assistance available?
- Is the checkout well staffed?
- Do queues form easily?
- Is the store easy to access and exit?
- Does the customer shop elsewhere and why?

The second type of customer, the browser or impulse purchaser, could be helped to make purchases by offering the following:

- Enough space to move around
- Plenty of rail space so that goods can be easily examined
- Attractive lighting
- Background staff, approaching customers can make them feel nervous and likely to leave
- Clearly displayed information

Finally, staff space should be considered. Sales assistants should have the room to move around without causing disruption to the consumer. Management should be clearly observed by the consumer, this will help promote the idea that the store is well organized.

THE IDEAL RETAIL ENVIRONMENT

There are two types of floor plan used by retailers:

- **Curved**   Customers are able to wander through the displays
- **Straight**   Where the goods almost meet the customer

At the beginning of a season the merchandiser will present the floor plan, giving a guide to where the different lines will be placed. The movement, or addition of stock, for example, swimwear which may be displayed later in the spring season, should also be shown. There may be a small mid-season sale and this will also have to be included. Usually there are several phases of presentation as new stock is introduced to keep customer attention.

The overall presentation should then be considered, beginning with the lighting. Lighting should be easy on the eye yet strong enough so that products can be seen, it can be used to focus customers' attention on certain products or lines.

The type of music played should suit the merchandise sold and the type of consumer. An older customer may like soft relaxing music while a younger customer may prefer louder music. Jean Jeanie identified its two main customers, the under 25s and the over 25s, they then observed the times these customers shopped, leading to a policy of different music to be played at these times to suit the customer.

Sales staff are part of the overall image. If corporate clothing is not worn then presentation should be stressed. If the store garments are worn then staff should be advised as to choice as this could help in the overall selling of goods. For example, some clothes do not have 'hanger' appeal, but if staff are seen wearing these items it may influence the customer to try them. Many companies are well aware of the importance of having a competent and well-trained staff and invest heavily on customer care programmes and give their staff up-to-date information on the goods they are selling. Unhelpful or disinterested staff can make the customer move on quickly.

SUMMARY

The introduction of computers into the distribution chain is providing manufacturer, retailer and consumer savings in both time and money.

The industry is constantly undergoing change as society changes, i.e. increased numbers of working mothers gives scope for the advancement of mail order and teleshopping systems. These systems are also ideal for an increasing older population.

Finally, the increased use of EDI will enable close observation of consumer trends. This will lead to a better service for the customer and less expensive mistakes for the retailer.

DISCUSSION POINTS:

1 Imagine that you have a position as an allocator in a warehouse of a major label. What would your priorities be in allocating stock to one customer and not another? How would you satisfy the needs of the smaller retailer against those of the larger concern?
2 The high street versus the out-of-town development. Visit both and compare the marketplaces analysing the advantages and disadvantages to the consumer. Suggest ways in which they could both be improved.
3 How do systems such as EDI and EPOS help the manufacturer and the retailer think of ways in which the marketing planner can best utilize this information?
4 In designing a shop floor for both a multiple store and a department store, explain how over a season you would make changes and draw up a timescale of when these changes would take place.

Chapter 7

The fashion calendar and the role of the buyer

This chapter concerns itself with the movement of fashion and the role of the buyer. In order to understand the role of the buyer it is useful to have an understanding of what is known as the fashion calendar.

THE FASHION CALENDAR

The aim of the calendar is to show the timing of design, production, distribution and retail over a twelve-month period. It will be useful to refer to Figure 7.1 to gain an overview of the calender.

Design collections

The collections are designed up to a year ahead. Take spring/summer collections as the example; while the previous year's garments are being retailed, the next year's ideas are being created, enabling both designer and buyer to observe any particular trends popular with the consumer that could be continued next year. If, say, loose-style T-shirts and ethnic prints have proved to be popular one summer, similar ideas can be used for the next summer's collection. At the end of the selling period for spring/summer the next year's design collections will be ready for show.

Production

Provisional arrangements will have been made during the designing of the collections. Many larger stores require their first delivery of the spring/summer collections in January. While customers are in the store for the winter sales, they can be attracted to the new collections, therefore production must begin during November and December. January and February will be the heaviest and most stressful production months of the season. During March/April the last of the orders will be completed. If there are any repeat orders because lines have sold well then these will be produced at this time.

Distribution

The correct timing and allocation of products is essential to the retail chain. As stated, distribution for spring/summer will begin in January, though smaller stores with less storage space may require stock later. All retailers will set manufacturers a deadline delivery date for first orders, usually around the end of April. Repeat orders can be placed in April but they must be distributed by the beginning of June.

Traditional selling times

These are most important for the retailer. During these periods trends can be observed which could help with the next year's choice. Retailers will complete weekly sales figures to monitor stock. Lines which are not selling can be removed from the shop floor to reappear at sale time. This will provide room for repeat orders.

Traditional sales times

At the end of a season it is important for the retailer to clear all stock. Prices are reduced and bargain packs organized to entice the consumer. If the economy is not good then it can appear as though the high street has a permanent sale. However, January and July are the main sales times, with the mid-season sales between.

Warehouse reductions

At the end of a production run, manufacturers find they have spare garments that have not been sold. There are generally two reasons for this. First, a production run is set to be cost effective, so although a manufacturer has orders say for 4,500 garments it may be just as cheap to produce 5,000 – this is known as achieving economies of scale. The spare garments can then be sold off. Second, if a retailer cancels orders or goes out of business then the manufacturer will be left with the garments. Retailers find warehouse reductions useful; if certain lines have been popular they can be purchased cheaper yet still be sold at the original price to the consumer, thus the retailers will achieve higher profit margins. If stock is running low retailers can restock cheaply. This stock can also be put into the sale (providing it has been on sale at a higher price for 30 days) at the end of a season.

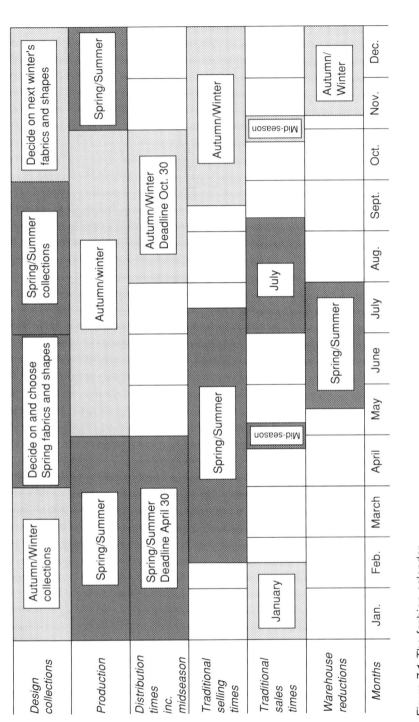

Figure 7.1 The fashion calendar

FASHION MARKETING TERMS

Outlined briefly below are some of the terms that are used specifically with regard to fashion marketing. It is useful to relate these terms to the fashion product life cycle in Chapter 5.

Trickle down

The original theory known as trickle down or diffusion and adoption of fashion owes a lot to the research by Midgley and Wills. This states that fashion moves from those groups in a higher economic status to those in lower socio-economic groups. Fashion will naturally filter through as those in lower socio-economic groups continually seek higher status. There is of course a system in place which allows this to happen. At the designer collections, looks are presented, according to Martin Evans (1989), to fashion journalists (who edit ranges and pick the 'most likely'), to consumer opinion leaders and to early then late adopters. It also has to be remembered that the famous, rich and often titled attend these shows; the designers they patronize can also be important in the adoption theories, as consumers will identify with the famous and 'their' style.

The fashion journalists or buyers will select garments and consumers to suit. At this stage they are seeking the type of consumer who is prepared to try out a new style – for a style to be widely accepted it has to be given publicity. It is not easy to state what socio-economic background the adopters of fashion are from though it is generally agreed that they are young. Katz and Lazarfeld (1955) characterized fashion opinion leaders as young, gregarious and highish in status. Midgeley (1974), while also discovering opinion leaders to be young, stated that they come from both the top and bottom of the socio-economic scale.

One example of the trickle-down theory in action is as follows: Vivienne Westwood created the idea of a bra to be worn as outerwear, showing it originally over the top of dresses. Designer Jean Paul Gaultier took this concept and produced conical-shaped bra-top dresses much favoured by the pop star Madonna. The idea eventually filtered down to the high street in a much more conservative form, however, the basic shape and design of the bra-dress remained.

Trickle up

The adoption process can also work the other way: in other words, the fashion created on the street will be taken up by designers. It is well known that many French and Italian designers gain a lot of their inspiration by observing the fashion in the clubs and on the streets of London. Jean Paul Gaultier has produced a range of football-type shirts,

Hamnett 'created' ripped jeans. Probably the most famous example of the trickle-up theory (because of its inclusion in the Victoria and Albert museum) is the Zandra Rhodes punk dress of the 1970s. Punk fashion, created on the streets, often involved the ripping up of clothes and attaching them back together with chains and safety pins. This was produced at little cost as the clothes had usually been obtained from jumble sales or second-hand shops. Zandra Rhodes created her version of the little black dress using silk, designer rips with finished edges, delicate chains and a diamond-studded safety pin, with a price tag of £2,500.

Horizontal

Once a fashion idea is being worn by a small group it may well spread to a larger audience without it necessarily moving up or down. Known as the horizontal theory, the 'fashion' is adopted by people of the same type. Take, for example, office clothes, which are generally not designer: a dress code can begin, for example a style of tie or length of skirt, which does not have a direct bearing on fashion but is adopted and worn by all members of staff usually of the same grading. Teenagers will often adopt fashion horizontally. A look, which may be quite simple, such as wearing socks over tights or a particular type of school bag or satchel, will spread across a school.

Other terms describe the nature or type of fashion. These are generally defined as classics or fads.

Classics

Styles or designs which remain very similar but can be adapted are known as 'classics'. The Chanel suit is very much a classic, the essential elements being the cardigan-style jacket with trim. Chanel shows this jacket season after season in various forms yet it remains recognizable.

In order to add kudos to a product or design it is often termed a classic. Reading through a fashion magazine will often result in the term classic being applied to the white shirt, blue jeans, jodphurs, little black dress and many other items. The term classic is much used in fashion, primarily by marketers, because it sounds so much better than 'safe'!

Fad

The concept of a 'fad' seems almost non-existent and certainly undesirable, yet it is essential to the fashion life cycle. Fads are usually extreme and therefore do not filter across the whole of society. It is interesting to compare a fad to a classic. While the marketer will use the term classic as a positive attribute, the term fad is avoided. The marketer will use phrases such as 'the latest', 'fun' or 'whacky' to describe such items. They never last long, often just a season; sometimes produced in just one style, they will quickly be adapted.

The little shorts known as 'hot pants' of the 1970s are a good example of a fad, made popular again by actress/singer Kylie Minogue in the 1990s. Among a teenage/young-20s audience, they were only for the very slender, and as they had a limited market, many variations were produced to maintain interest.

THE ROLE OF THE BUYER IN FASHION MARKETING

The buyer has been called the essential link in the fashion marketing chain; for fashion to move from the catwalk or showroom floor to the retail outlet it has to be purchased. The buyer's job is often viewed as one of the most glamorous jobs in the fashion industry, with top buyers almost as well known as the designers of fashion. Clare Stubbs of Harrods, Amanda Verdan of Harvey Nichols and Joan Burnstein of Browns are among the most famous buyers.

Their role is to predict and buy what they feel will be the next season's fashion. They will often try to gain exclusive deals for their store from the most current designers. Their relationship with the designer is two-way; the store will gain the credibility of having stocked the 'in'-name designer and the 'in'-name designer will have secured sales and prestige by being stocked at a top-name store. Exclusive collections to stores also help with price control as occasionally designers' goods can appear discounted in other stores thus losing their exclusivity, a circumstance which is detrimental both to the designer and the store. Consequently, designers 'look after' the buyers, by assuring them the best seats at the catwalk shows and invitations to parties afterwards.

The life of the top buyer is hectic, attending all the international fashion shows and fashion/textile fairs, they control budgets running into millions and the next season's profits depend on their judgement. If a designer should suddenly lose credibility or the goods ordered do not fit properly then the store's customers will go elsewhere.

However, for most buyers the reality is much more mundane. Their sources are not the international designer shows, they will instead be reliant on the following:

- **Store records/past experience** Most companies will keep records of suppliers. These will contain details of specific items purchased.
- **Market representatives/agents** They provide an essential service for the smaller store as it is these retail outlets which cannot afford to visit all the trade shows. An agent will often act for several non-competing producers, i.e., knitwear, jewellery, ladies outer wear, evening wear,

and so on, and will therefore be able to offer a full selection to the retailer.

- **Competition** If a shop report reveals that a design/designer is selling well in another store then the producers can be contacted.
- **Magazines** Trade magazines such as *Drapers Record* provide weekly figures of top-selling items as well as forecast for the coming season. They also provide fashion features with details of the manufacturers. The magazines contain a directory listing manufacturers which is a useful source of information. Fashion magazines such as *Vogue, Elle* and *ID* and general magazines such as *Marie Claire, Cosmopolitan* and *New Woman* are also good guides for the buyer.
- **Recommendations** Using information from other buyers in the company, a buyer can check reliability of time schedules and quality of manufacturers.
- **Trade directories** These are classified lists of wholesalers and manufacturers. Regularly up-dated, they provide a convenient list of the resources available. *The Cloth Directory* is an example of a trade directory.
- **Visits to trade shows and exhibitions** If the retailer can afford it this will be an invaluable source of information. In Britain, the smaller retailer has found Harrogate to be a valuable source.
- **Films/exhibitions/shows** Many people are influenced by the way celebrities dress or are dressed. The grunge look was worn both by film stars and pop stars, this look was copied by designers.

Once the information has been gathered the buyer must then consider the following:

- **Planning and programming** A timetable and allocation programme has to be developed. This will involve the setting of delivery dates, arranging the movement of stock, particularly if the company has a central warehouse, and the financing of all operations.
- **Buying in** Is the actual purchase of stock, the buyer will use the following criteria for selecting goods:

    Suitability of merchandise
    Profitability of merchandise
    Client and customer services
    Reliability of resource
    Convenience of resource

    The buyer also needs to know if the supplier is local, which would make trade arrangements easier. Does the stock have a well-known brand name? Is the manufacturer undertaking any marketing?
- **Budgeting** The finances have to be set for the buyer. This usually involves setting the OTB or open-to-buy figure and a model stock plan.

Open to buy is the amount available for the purchase of new stock; **Model stock plan** is the translation of the budget giving prices, sizes, colours and amounts of stock.

The methods involved in calculating these are explained later.

- **Contract**   The buyer will organize contracts for all suppliers. Goods must meet with the requirements of the Sale of Goods Act. Contract also includes the negotiation of price, delivery dates and discounts.
- **Promotions**   When a new season begins, joint promotions with other departments can prove to be cost effective when attracting customers. For example, a fashion show in a department store would use several different styles of fashion garments, accessories and cosmetics. If there is an in-house hair/beauty salon this can also be promoted.

Buying from abroad

The purchase of goods from foreign suppliers is widespread. This will become more prevalent as the single European market comes into effect. Foreign goods are often cheaper compared to British products, usually because of the availability of cheaper materials and labour. A much better quality for the price can be achieved. This can offer the possibilities of higher mark-ups for the buyer.

Some foreign brands, particularly Italian and French, are viewed as prestigious. Other countries have reputations for producing lower quality but cheaper goods such as Portugal or India. When buying from abroad the buyer has to be aware that:

- Imported merchandise may be subject to tariffs.
- The cost of goods can vary depending on the strength or weakness of the pound.
- Time has to be allowed for distribution, particularly if goods are being shipped in.
- If there are any variations in quality it is more difficult to return the goods.
- Re-ordering can prove problematic because of time for delivery.
- Sizes and shapes alter from country to country, assurances must be made that these are correct for the home audience.

THE BUYER AND THE BUDGET

Once the buyer has been given a budget and sales have been predicted then the OTB or open-to-buy calculations will be made. This will give the amounts of money to be spent to achieve required stock levels and therefore sales target at any given time over the season. It is first necessary to understand the general terms and the formulas that are used.

Average stock

The average estimated stock sales for a given period is divided by the amount of times the stock should turn-over (rate of stock-turn, RST) or to put it another way the number of times stock has to be replaced.

$$\frac{\text{Estimated sales (total)}}{\text{RST}} = \text{average stock}$$

Average sales

A simple average is found when estimated sales are divided by the number of months in the period. In the fashion industry this can vary, but if budgeting for the year it will be 12.

$$\frac{\text{Estimated sales (total)}}{\text{'12'}} = \text{average sales}$$

Basic stock

In order to offer the consumer a selection of goods there has to be a minimum amount in store, the formula for finding this basic stock is:

$$\text{average stock} - \text{average sales} = \text{basic stock}$$

Opening stock

On the first day of each calculated month there will be a planned amount of stock:

$$\text{estimated sales (month)} + \text{basic stock} = \text{opening stock}$$

Closing stock

This is the amount of stock that is planned for the last day of the month and the amount will be the same as the calculated opening stock.

Markdowns

These are goods that have had to be reduced, because of buying errors, selling errors, weather, damaged goods, or prices set too high originally. The usual types of markdown are as follows:

- **Carryover**   Occasionally the markdown required to sell is so high that it is worth the merchandiser considering storing the goods until the next season when the goods may then be sold at their 'true' price. There are several disadvantages:

  1 Storage of goods can be expensive and the transportation, warehousing (labour and insurance) and reticketing will all cost.
  2 Goods tend to become damaged and can gain a shop-soiled appearance.
  3 Money tied up in the goods cannot be released until they are sold thus meaning that the shop may find it difficult to purchase enough new stock to keep customers interested.
  4 Some customers may remember the goods from the previous year which will not enhance the shop's image as a fashion store.

- **Early markdown**   Some retailers will markdown goods that are not selling as soon as possible. There are three main reasons for this:

  1 Any sale of goods will provide capital to buy more popular lines thus increasing turnover.
  2 In fashion the beginning of a season usually finds customers at their most interested in purchasing; a markdown, therefore, might provide an extra temptation.
  3 Having one large end-of-season sale often provides extra staff costs in overtime and additional personnel.

- **Late markdown**   There are just as many reasons for justifying late markdowns, for example:

  1 Some lines are slow starters. For example, while a store may stock a sleeveless shirt in February, in the UK because of the weather it will not be bought until, say, May.
  2 Markdowns can have a detrimental effect on the other stock in store making it look expensive and the customer could question that. A store does lose prestige by having constant sales.
  3 If a customer realizes that the shop marks goods down, say, every six weeks they will often wait for that period to make their purchase.

- **Automatic markdown**   Some stores have a policy of high turnover so, if stock has not moved off the shelf in, say, three weeks, it will be reduced as a matter of policy. This is usually the case in the retailer selling to the younger teenage market.

Buying commitments

As goods will often be on order during any selling period then the money to pay for these goods always has to be taken into consideration.

Open to buy

To arrive at the open-to-buy figure first you need to calculate the following:

- estimated sales
- closing stocks
- markdown allocation

When you have calculated this figure it needs to be subtracted from the value of goods already allocated according to the model stock plan. You must also take into account:

- opening stock
- buying commitments

Situation

A small independent store would like to purchase some hats to go with the summer collection. In order to do this the manager needs to find the OTB, her estimated sales for the month are £15,000. The shop began the month with £18,000 of stock and plans to have a closing stock of £10,000. An estimated markdown figure of 7 per cent against sales has been allocated and she has buying commitments of £6,000 for the month.

Estimated sales	15,000		
Closing stock	10,000		
Markdowns	1,500		
		TOTAL	26,500
Opening stock	18,000		
Buying commitments	6,000		
		TOTAL	24,000
	OTB		2,500

This gives the open to buy at selling price, to find the actual amount she can spend the profit margin needs to be found, for this example we will assume the margin is 65 per cent.

65% of 2,500 =	1,625
2,500 − 1,625 =	875

This means that she has £875 available to spend on purchasing hats.

Model stock plan

This will be devised using the OTB calculation to determine how much money is available for stock, past store records for information of previous sales and size requirements and where possible market research.

The model stock plan will then take account of size, colour and co-ordination of goods. For example, a teenage shop may stock with an emphasis on sizes 8 to 14, a shop for those aged 25–40 will buy more heavily sizes 12 to 16.

When a buyer is determining a plan it is always useful to work with the merchandiser, who is the person responsible for the selling of goods. The merchandiser will have a better understanding of how the goods will appear in the store, this is useful for colour and co-ordination.

Table 7.1 Example of a model stock plan

Style no	Size 8	10	12	14	16	Colour	Price	Totals (£)
85061	2	4	8	8	6	Saphire	£12.99	363.72
85062	0	2	6	6	4	Ochre	£18.99	341.82
85063	0	0	0	0	0	–	–	–
85064	3	4	10	10	8	Stripes	£16.99	594.65
85054	2	4	6	6	4	Taupe	£18.99	417.78
85054	2	4	8	8	8	Black	£18.99	569.70
Totals	9	18	38	38	30			£1,300.19

Table 7.1 is an example of what part of a model stock plan could look like for a shop catering for the 25–40 year-old women.

The function of buying is to generate profit. The following theory has been put forward by Jack Sugden. In devising model stock plans and in the buying process, it is said that the buyer assumes four different roles:

- **Change agent**   This is the person who influences key decisions thought necessary by the company. A change agent would also influence consumer purchasing decisions and the supplier.
- **Gatekeeper**   Here a person controls the goods from the manufacturer to the consumer by selecting those most appropriate to the needs, wants and desires of the consumer.
- **Opinion leader**   As a source of advice and information the buyer can influence the decision-making processes of the consumer.
- **Innovator**   This involves the high risk of taking products without any knowledge of their sellability.

As the buyer has to source the right goods at the right price for the right consumer, so the merchandiser has to sell the right goods at the right price to the right consumer. The merchandiser will be directly involved in matters concerning price, quality levels and style as well as determining calculations such as markdowns. Many of the merchandiser's activities are discussed in Chapter 9.

SUMMARY

The fashion production process is on a continual cycle from which trends can be observed. The information taken from previous sales records can prove invaluable in determining a buying policy for the season.

Buyers have to be aware of the movement of fashion; today's street look could be tomorrow's couture and vice versa. The adoption of fashion by groups also has to be taken into account, although this is explored more fully in Chapter 2.

The buyer and the merchandiser are said to be involved in:

- selection of goods
- advertising
- pricing
- timescaling
- sales force training/selection

For this they require:

- solid education
- analytical skills
- enthusiasm
- communication skills
- product knowledge
- objective reasoning
- leadership skills

DISCUSSION POINTS

1 You are about to begin a budget to show to the bank manager which details when you will need to buy stock for your shop. Explain what your buying policies will be.
2 The company has decided that it would like to diversify into the teenage market. How would you go about sourcing the goods?
3 Imagine you have a budget of £50,000. Draw up a model stock plan

for a menswear shop catering for the male aged 30–44, social class ABC1.

4 Visit three different types of retail outlet and observe what, if any, markdowns they have. Try to ascertain when and how often they have sales. Compare each outlet taking these factors into account.

Chapter 8

Pricing and payments; strategies and methods

THE SIGNIFICANCE OF PRICING FOR THE FASHION MARKETER

Pricing plays a vital role in fashion marketing because it is the only part of the marketing mix which contributes to profit; the product, distribution and promotion simply add to the costs. It is important in the company's overall strategy because the strength of the company is measured in financial terms, whether it is profit, turnover, or return on capital employed.

Although costs play a key role in fashion pricing, it is important to understand that costs are not the only determinant of successful pricing. The price charged will also need to reflect the type of fashion items on offer and where that product is positioned. People are prepared to pay more for a pair of Armani jeans than a pair of Marks and Spencer jeans, even though they may not perceive much difference in the actual product once it is removed from the selling environment.

Pricing also needs to be considered in the context of the marketing mix as a whole: choice of an exclusive distributor such as Harvey Nichols or Harrods will carry with it the implication of premium pricing. On the other hand, normally premium-priced designer wear is sometimes made available at lower than normal prices as a promotional exercise.

Traditionally, pricing in the fashion manufacturing industry has been cost-orientated, with consumer pricing being seen as the domain of the retailer. The increase in international competition is now encouraging fashion marketers to concentrate their attention on the pricing issue.

PRICING AND COSTS

Costs of production or selling play an important role in developing the price of garments. Many firms still employ a cost-based approach to pricing, in which the costs of production are first established and then profits are decided on the basis of this information. At its most basic level, pricing bears little relation to what customers are prepared to pay: customers may be prepared to pay much more for a garment, alternatively, far larger numbers of a particular style could be sold if it were priced differently.

Before we go on to explain all the problems involved in setting prices in the fashion industry, and the relationship between costs and prices, we will explain some of the basic terminology.

Gross margin

In order to achieve a price for an item the level of gross margin should first be set. Gross margin is the gross profit expressed as a percentage of the selling price.

For example, if the cost price of a pack of socks was £2.00 and the selling price was £2.50, then:

$$\text{Gross margin} = \frac{2.50 - 2.00}{\times 100}$$

$$= 0.50 \times 100$$

$$= 20\%$$

The gross margin in this case is set at 20 per cent.

Average gross margin

Not all items are sold or produced using the same gross margin. Items which can be sold quickly will have a lower gross margin; the same could be true of items which are cheaper to produce.

It is important for a business to be able to find the average gross margin, that is the gross margin averaged out across all goods either retailed or produced.

For example, if the cost price of the goods sold in a given period was £50,032 and the overall selling price was £58,936 then:

$$\text{Average Gross margin} = \frac{£58,936 - £50,032}{\times 100}$$

$$= £8,904 \times 100$$

$$= 15.1\%$$

The gross margin for individual items, therefore could range between, say, 12 per cent and 35 per cent depending on the width and depth of the range of products stocked.

Fixed expenses/costs

Such expenses are usually the least difficult to discover. If relying on last year's budget, then it is wise to increase it by the current rate of inflation. Fixed expenses are those which remain the same regardless of levels of production or retail. They include rents, business tax, insurance, loans and professional charges.

Variable expenses/costs

Unlike fixed expenses, these will vary with the amount of output. If, for example, a retailer was selling well, then this would involve more administration, a higher investment in new stock and maybe the employment and training of staff. Other variable expenses include heating/lighting, transport, advertising and telephone bills.

Semi-variable expenses/costs

While some costs will be termed variables, individually they could also alter. The employment of staff can create semi-variable expenses. The nature of the fashion retail industry demands increased labour at certain times, before Christmas, for example. Some staff could be working on a basic-plus-commission basis and this too would be included as a semi-variable expense. In the manufacture the company may offer short-term employment for students over the summer period or bonuses may be given to machinists; these too will count as semi-variable.

COSTING SYSTEMS AND PROCEDURES FOR THE MANUFACTURER

Manufacturers usually operate a basic cost plus pricing or standard mark-up system. This works well if orders remain constant. If there are sudden fluctuations in size of orders or if a different production technique is developed then a more accurate and reliable system needs to be employed. The manufacturer should consider the following:

- **Product pricing**
- **Purchase of raw materials, choice of suppliers**
- **Production volume**
- **Wages (including piecework, overtime)**

- Production facility increases and decreases
- Purchase of capital equipment

For every production run the set-up costs must be calculated if the correct profit margins are to be achieved. These calculations should not be based on order size but should consider the following:

- **Difficulties of the new product**
- **New techniques to be developed**
- **Training for new machinery**
- **Operators learning times**

The costs for these should be added to the overall cost of the production run. To help with these calculations, records of previous job costings, taking into account the above, should be kept, these can then become the basis for current costings.

As the clothing industry is labour intensive, it is the cost of operators learning new techniques or a different operation that should be identified. This can be shown through the payroll. Most operators work piecework (they are paid for each piece they complete) and the times taken can be calculated, therefore, and production efficiencies thus observed. It can be useful to draw up learning or experience curves to understand the costs of the following:

- **Line efficiency**
- **Operator efficiency**
- **Average and marginal costs**
- **Labour costs for standard and non-standard operations**

These can then be transferred to a costing sheet. The costing sheet should have its origins in the design room, giving details of fabric, trimmings, labels and include an approximate price. From this, a production costing sheet can be formulated with:

- **Calculations of labour costs including pattern and pre-production costs**
- **Standard operations split into piece work, i.e. overlock, shoulder seams, etc.**
- **Non-standard operations again split into piece work**
- **Total material costs**
- **Fixed order costs to cover administration**
- **Direct costs (materials and labour)**
- **Indirect costs overheads**
- **Gross margin required**

The sales price can then be determined.

PRICING OBJECTIVES AND STRATEGIES

We have already mentioned that costs are only one of the considerations involved in pricing in the fashion industry. Price setting also involves considering the needs of the consumer, the company's corporate objectives and the activities of the competition. The main elements involved in the pricing decision are thus:

- **Costs**
- **Customers**
- **Company**
- **Competition**

We will consider pricing from two perspectives; companies already established in the market, and companies entering a new market.

A company which is already established in the market, for example the Sears group, could have as its objectives:

- **Expansion**   The company may wish to expand its market share, sales or profits.
- **Competition**   Lower prices may be set to compete with either current competition or threats from new companies entering the market.
- **Generation of cash**   The company may be considering new ventures or relocation. Cash will need to be recovered quickly.
- **Maximize profitability**   Either short- or long-term on investments or current capital employed.

A company entering the market, such as Kookaï, will have other objectives to consider such as:

- **Customer awareness**   Prices can be set together with another objective such as quality. Marks and Spencer, for example, has a reputation for quality knitwear at a more affordable price than most high street fashion stores, thus their customers feel they receive value for money.
- **Competition**   In the face of competition from existing suppliers/ retailers, the company may place an emphasis on product rather than price in order to secure a market positioning.
- **Return on investment**   The company will need to show financiers or shareholders that their product sales are in line with cash-flow forecasts.

Once the pricing objectives have been clearly determined the external and internal factors should be considered as these may add costs to the price.

External economic factors

The marketing manager will always need to bear in mind the PESTEL factors as discussed in Chapter 2, but some external economic factors also have an important influence on pricing as follows:

- **Inflation** This has the effect of increasing costs and the monetary value of sales, as pricing must be over and above the rate of inflation. Companies should also be aware that inflation does not just affect themselves. Suppliers' prices will also rise and customers may not be able to afford goods as interest rates will be affected. A high rate of inflation causing interest rates to rise is one of the main reasons for bankruptcy or liquidation in fashion companies.
- **The economic cycle** If the economy is bad this can lead to a depression or recession. The economies of other countries should be considered. A country undergoing either a boom or depression will have a similar effect on those countries it trades with. The opposite is also true: when an economy is growing there are possibilities for widespread job and wealth creation.
- **Changes in local conditions** While new shopping developments such as Thurrock Lakeside can present opportunities to larger retail companies, they can also have a knock-on effect in killing off traditional high street shops.

Internal economic factors

- **Size of the premises** Will they be large enough to accommodate stock or should the company relocate?
- **State of the premises** Does money need to be spent on refurbishing or on new equipment?
- **Staff** What are the current requirements for the company? Will any training or retraining programmes need to be initiated?
- **Sales promotion/advertising** If the brand to be sold is unknown then this could add a significant cost to the budget.

PRICING METHODS

The final price selected will also depend on whether the company decides to base its offering solely on costs or to use a marketing-based method, or some combination of the two.

Cost-based pricing methods

Cost-based pricing methods in the fashion industry will be modified by the following factors:

- Manufacturers' recommended prices
- Trade prices guides
- Competitors' prices
- Gross profit margin required

From this point a mixture of methods may be chosen as is shown below:

- **Standard mark-up pricing**   Once the actual cost of the product has been determined then a percentage mark-up is added. It does not consider other factors such as:

  Advertisers'/marketing costs
  Competitors' prices
  Marginal costs

  This method is frequently used, with the result that the price of the goods to the retailer will be doubled for the consumer. For example, a hat priced at £8.50 will be sold by the retailer for £17.00. The manufacturer or wholesaler will often recommend a selling price to try to ensure consistency.
- **Target pricing**   Price is determined using the estimated sales volume. The amount of sales therefore determine the price regardless of other factors. This method is best used for smaller items such as hosiery or for high-fashion 'fad' items.
- **Demand-orientated pricing**   To encourage goods to sell quickly, operating lower profit margins could prove effective. Goods which do not move quickly can be priced higher to compensate for a longer shelf life.
- **Stabilization pricing**   During periods of high inflation/interest rates the costs of production, distribution and retail can increase rapidly. A price for garments will be set at the beginning of a season. Any changes in costs will result in lower profit margins.

Marketing-based pricing methods

Marketing-based pricing will not only consider costs, but some of the objectives of the company which were discussed earlier, such as the need to generate cash, and above all the needs of the consumer. Pricing in the fashion industry is more complex than in the FMCG sector, because of the way the industry is structured. The standard methods of establishing a price level are:

- **Market skimming**   This is when the price is set high while a product is new to the market in order to maximize profits.
- **Market penetration**   Prices are set low in order to sell as many as possible and establish a larger market share.

Taking the industry as a whole, the designer section of the fashion industry is forever using the skimming method, because it only has a short time in which to sell to an exclusive group of clients before the garment enters the mass market and loses its prestige. Alternatively, as far as marketing to the consumer is concerned, market penetration pricing is the most commonly used method. Industry-to-industry pricing actually offers companies some scope for flexibility in their pricing methods, but this is the very area in which cost-based pricing dominates.

Marketing-based pricing methods most commonly used when marketing direct to the consumer are:

- **Psychological pricing**
- **Price lining**
- **Competitor-based pricing**

We explain each of these approaches to pricing below:

- **Psychological pricing**   There are two basic concepts at work here: prestige and value.

  Prestige pricing works on the basis that to make an item exclusive and therefore more desirable a higher price must be charged. It is the label of the product that becomes important to the fashion-conscious consumer, the label is what differentiates them from other wearers of fashion. Purchasing a 'label' has now been called 'investment dressing', a phrase coined to detract from the obvious conspicuous consumption that occurs when, for example, an Armani dress with a price tag of £3,500 is purchased. With a higher price tag customers will expect more in terms of customer service, such as having the garment specially packaged.

  Some labels are prestigious even though they are not beyond the reach of the ordinary person but just slightly more costly than alternatives. For example, Levi 501 jeans have gained a place as a classic worn by the fashionable of all ages. Prestige is gained by those wearing the jeans, they are sending out a message.

  The aim of value pricing is to ensure that the customer feels she is gaining value for money when making a purchase. This could be an individual item such as a silk blouse priced £19.99, the value coming from the fact that the item is silk and the price low.

Two further aspects of pricing would come under the umbrella of psychological pricing. The first is multiple packs, such as items of children's clothing, underwear and hosiery, which offer a reduction on what they would cost if bought separately. This approach has an added advantage of preventing customers from buying elsewhere in the meantime as they have purchased sufficient quantities to last. The cheque guarantee card factor is the second aspect. The most widely used cheque guarantee cards often still have a limit of £50.00. Retailers require additional proof of identity for prices over this amount. Price-sensitive customers will use the limit as a spending barrier, being reluctant to go over the limit. For some retailers it would be wise to price just under £50.00 and accept a lower profit margin.

- **Price lining**   Ranges will be priced so a variety of different styles can be found within similar price brackets. This helps to entice the price-sensitive consumer. Once the consumer has decided on a certain price then concentration can be on selection rather than looking at price tags. Prices are usually clearly displayed, there may be four different price brackets for one type of garment, such as a range of shirts priced at £17.99, £19.99, £21.99 and £24.99. As the prices are close to one another the consumer will not feel cheated in moving to another bracket.
- **Competition-orientated pricing**   In some sections of the fashion market, competition plays an important role in establishing the price. Take, for example, the target group of the 25–44 year-old woman in social classes B, C1, C2. There are several high street chains offering similar styles: Next, Principles, Marks and Spencer, and so on. The labels are not a priority in customer choice; value for money is. It is important therefore, that price is competitive if manufacturers/retailers are to secure custom.

CUSTOMER PURCHASE AND PRICE

It is becoming apparent that the method of customer purchase is vital to promoting loyalty and increasing market share. Once goods have been selected, the customer usually wants to leave the store as quickly and conveniently as possible. Few customers use cash; among the over 18s, cheques or credit cards are the more popular options. Payment by debit card such as Switch offers customers another choice (this takes money direct from the customer's bank account) but this particular method does not offer the retailer many opportunities.

Credit cards

The credit card offers much to the retailers, however, there is increasing competition between brand names, building societies and stores' own cards. While Access and Visa are international and the issuing banks can offer additional services, their interest rates are higher than building societies. Despite this, the building societies 'low-interest' cards have not had a geat response. They have tried to offer 'added value' alongside the low interest. Added value has included a percentage to be given to named charities, cash rebates on amounts spent annually and interest paid on credit balances. It appears that the consumer's priority, however, is whether they can pay the monthly amount rather than the interest.

Store cards

Store cards or retailer credit cards could be one answer to declining customer spending. As banks issuing credit cards are now demanding an annual fee for their use, and retailers too are allowed to charge for the use of credit cards, the store card could be a much more attractive proposition for the consumer. The advantages for the retailer are that store cards allow for the creation of customer databases, this information can then be used to sell other goods and services. If retailers only accept usage of their own card, as is the case with Marks and Spencers, then they have a captive audience and can build on this relationship. It is the innovative development of cards (there are already many types) that will give retailers the ability to fight off competition.

Group cards

Companies such as Burton's, Sears and Storehouse issue group cards which can be used at any of their outlets. This ensures a loyalty to the group and allows for inter-group promotion.

The Goldbergs started the Style card now operated by the Royal Bank of Scotland. Card users are able to use the services of other non-competing retailers such as travel agencies, tyre and exhaust centres. While this method has the advantage of reaching a wider clientele it also means that the individual company's profiles are lowered.

Affinity cards

Access and Visa issuers began this type of card where users can be linked to trade unions, sports organizations or, as discussed earlier, charities. According to Steve Worthington this approach could be used by retailers too:

> to support regional or local campaigns because of their capacity to distinguish the credit transactions by outlet and also because of their ability to communicate different messages to card holders in different geographical locations.

He also suggests that international retailers such as Laura Ashley or Benetton could be affinity users of Visa or Mastercard.

There is another group of cards which in some way offer the customer financial rewards for use.

Discount cards

This type of card was first issued by Mothercare in mid-1988. Customers pay an annual fee and are then entitled to discount on all purchases. Once customers have paid their fee they are obviously going to want a return on the investment and this ensures sales for the retailer. If the retailer can provide sufficient quality and choice then there is the opportunity to build up brand and store loyalty. The discount card system relies on regular purchases in order to make it work both for the retailer and customer. Identifying sections of the market where regular purchases are made could provide the retailer with more users for this type of card.

Cardholder discount

The larger retail store groups who offer umbrella cards, such as Burtons and Sears, will give discounts. These can either be on selected stores or items and are available for limited time periods. As only cardholders are entitled to the discounts, the method allows retailers to build on customer loyalty and the chance to promote the store/group card.

Payment option/deferred payment option

These cards appear to give the customer more control over their finances. Payment option allows the customer reduced interest charges by paying off the monthly balance. It was introduced by the American store group Daytons as 'credit on your terms' to entice those customers nervous about credit card use. The fact that interest rates are not fixed gives the payment option card the appearance of being customer friendly.

A deferred payment option can allow customers up to three months interest-free credit. This means that if customers pay off the full amount within the set period no interest charges will be incurred. With Access and Visa cards shopping has to be carefully timed to avoid charges and the time span is not so long. The deferred payment option would take this pressure away from the consumer.

Rebate cards

A rebate card entitles consumers to a percentage of the money spent to be rebated. The more money spent the higher the percentage of rebate. For the retailer this provides opportunities to build up customer loyalty to the store. This method is useful for both peak- and low-selling periods. During the peak period of November to December customers will be more likely to use the store issuing a rebate card in the knowledge that by doing all their shopping at one place they will gain greater discounts. For the retailer, the card could be promoted during slow-selling periods to increase customer flow and spending.

Future methods of purchase

The method of purchase that is presently undergoing development is teleshopping. It has been used successfully by catalogue companies in Britain since the launch of the *Next Directory*. For the customer, purchase can be made quickly and conveniently without having to fill out order forms. If it is backed up with a fast delivery service, this method is ideal for many sections of the market from the elderly or disabled to the working mother or busy executive.

British Telecom will provide the system which the teleshopping consortium will use. It will begin with train and air tickets, moving to durable goods and finally food shopping. The expense of these systems has so far prevented retailers from developing teleshopping. As systems become more advanced and communication systems use television screens to display current information, systems which can be accessed by consumers with their own home terminal could become an attractive proposition.

SUMMARY

Historically, pricing in the fashion industry has been dominated by the cost-based approach, particularly in the manufacturing sector. A marketing-based approach to pricing is an effective way of matching what the company can achieve to customers' requirements.

Costs cannot be ignored, particularly when prices are set for a whole season, irrespective of whether the manufacturer may face unexpected increases in costs. In the fashion industry in particular, therefore, cost control may be the only effective means of retaining profit levels.

The retailer in direct competition has little choice but to follow competitors' prices. Guidelines are usually provided by the manufacturer/wholesaler. It is therefore important that the retailer considers the effect of fixed and variable costs on the gross profit margin. Once the running costs for the outlet have been calculated, sales figures should then be estimated. If the amount of sales will not cover the running costs or the margins are too low then the retailer may have to consider the following:

● less staff
● different brand with less competition
● relocation

Carefully calculated running costs, the keeping of sales analysis figures containing opening stock, intake and sales will help to prevent any catastrophies. The most important factor to consider is that pricing must be looked at not only from the cost perspective but from the customer perspective too.

DISCUSSION POINTS

1 You are in the process of producing a new range of clothing for a well-established company. Explain what pricing strategies you would use.
2 An independent fashion store is establishing itself on a high street which includes the most famous multiples. The independent store stocks some designer labels as well as stock which is similar to that of the multiple. What advice would you give regarding pricing policies and future stock purchase?
3 As the area manager of a multiple chain which does not operate its own card but accepts Access/Visa/Mastercard you have been asked to give advice to senior management on the viability of offering an in-store card. Give an account of the options available.
4 Market research for a fashion company has shown that the skirts are not selling well, yet a competitor is offering a different style and that has almost sold out! The factory is mid-way through production, what price factors would you consider if you were to change designs?

Chapter 9

Promotion in the fashion industry

THE PURPOSE OF PROMOTING FASHION

Some fashions seem to spread without any active promotion on the part of the company, particularly among innovators (experimenters) and the early adopters (trendsetters). However, at particular points in the economic cycle, such as times of recession, companies need to adopt a more proactive stance if they are to succeed.

For most fashion companies, the key to attracting attention and custom from both the trendsetters and from the mainstream consumer market is through promotions. The main purpose of promotion is to act as the firm's mouthpiece, to 'inform and persuade' the customer.

THE PREREQUISITES OF PROMOTING FASHION

Underlying any fashion promotions plan is an understanding of consumers' buying behaviour and of the adoption process. Even though a high proportion of many companies' promotional budgets are still spent on business-to-business promotions (e.g. manufacturers to retailers) the increasing importance of brand awareness and quality issues means that the consumer cannot be overlooked.

Essentially, the fashion marketer must bear in mind that promotional strategies must be changed as a particular fashion moves through the adoption cycle. What will be an appropriate promotions strategy when a fashion is first introduced will not be appropriate if the company is competing for market share in the mainstream market.

Fashion marketers need to take account of consumer behaviour when segmenting and targeting the market, so that both message and media can be targeted effectively. Additionally, understanding the actual buying process is important for fine-tuning the promotions schedule.

The relationship between promotions choice and the decision-making process becomes apparent if we take the basic 'AIDA' model:

Awareness	The customer must become aware of the existence of a style, often through fashion magazines.
Interest	The customer is interested in more information about the style.
Desire	The customer is involved in an active product search, e.g. for stockists, and evaluation of products, e.g. pricing.
Action	Actual purchase and trial of the garment.

Each stage requires a different level of communication, since the customer has different information needs, and this is the task facing the fashion marketer; which methods of promotion to use, which promotions policy to adopt and how to use the promotions.

UNDERSTANDING PROMOTIONS

Promotion is all about communicating with the customer and the wider public. Before we examine the individual promotional tools that the fashion marketer can use, it is important to understand the communication process.

Most of the ideas about the communication process are derived from military uses, but are equally applicable to retailing where poor communication can result in loss of customers, loss of business and lost jobs for those who work in the industry.

In Figure 9.1, the sender will be the fashion company, and the encoder will be those entrusted to design and send the necessary message to the consumer, for example an advertising or PR agency. Decoding the message involves interpreting the ideas contained in the message, the receiver being the actual customer or others in the wider public. The noise represents the distractions that surround the message which can distort it, in the same way that interference can affect a television transmission. Understanding the communications process helps in developing promotional programmes and also in interpreting competitor activity.

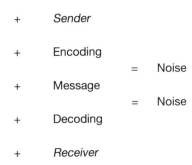

Figure 9.1 The basic communications model

The classic example from the fashion industry of the communications process at work is that of the controversial series of advertisements run by Benetton featuring pictures such as that of a young man dying of AIDS. Many of these advertisements created a furore. Benetton maintained that their message was aimed at a particular target group (i.e. the receivers) who would interpret the message in a different way to the general public.

METHODS OF PROMOTION AND PROMOTIONS POLICIES

There are four main types of promotions, collectively referred to as the promotions mix:

- Advertising
- Sales promotion
- Publicity
- Personal selling

How they are used depends to a great extent on the marketing strategy and promotions policy which the company adopts. In the past, the UK fashion industry has concentrated heavily on publicity and personal selling as the preferred promotions methods. Competitive pressure from other European and US companies which have incorporated growing brand awareness, and the increasingly inner-directedness of the consumer into their marketing strategies, is now creating waves in the UK fashion

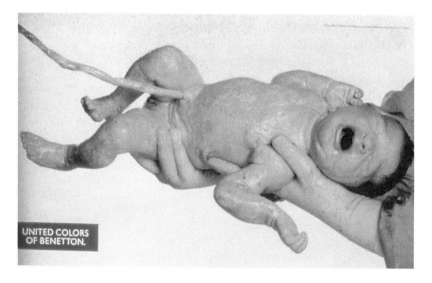

Plate 9.1 One of Benetton's most controversial advertisements

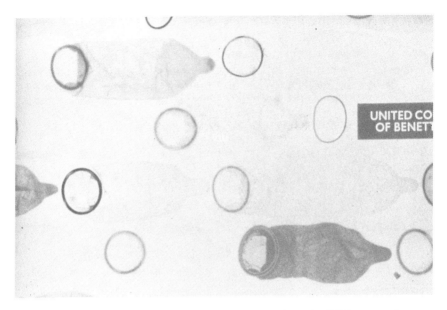

Plate 9.2 The 'condom' advertisement for Benetton's early 1990s campaign

industry's promotions policies. There are two basic types of promotions policies, or strategies:

- **Push strategy**   This approach concentrates all promotion efforts on the distribution channel.
- **Pull strategy**   Using this method promotion is directed towards the consumer.

Push

The 'push' policy has been traditionally favoured by UK fashion marketers; the focus of promotion has been on the nearest link in the distribution chain, be it wholesaler or retailer. This has resulted in a bias towards personal selling and publicity aimed at the trade press, particularly around the time of shows.

Pull

Competitors from the international arena have made inroads by utilizing a 'pull' policy to sustain their strategy of creating strong brand images. Advertising and sales promotions coupled with more adventurous use of PR are used to stimulate demand for products.

Each element in the communications mix will now be explained in more detail in the following sections.

ADVERTISING

Advertising is the most visible part of the fashion company's promotional activities. It is a non-personal form of communication that is seen by a far wider public than just the company's own customers, as the use of posters on London buses by The Gap will testify.

Despite its importance as a promotional tool, advertising is still not widely used by UK manufacturers, who spend about one-third of their European competitor's typical advertising budgets. The fashion industry is the UK's fourth biggest industry but not one company appears in the Top 10 advertising spenders noted in *Marketing* magazine.

Advertising plays a key role in the consumer decision-making process: it can create product or brand awareness, build up image, provide information for decision making and also influence post-purchase behaviour. The relationship between advertising and other consumer goods is very different to that between advertising and fashion. Advertising helps to build up the product image, and particularly when buying fashion, consumers are buying an image. Creating a misleading image can have a seriously damaging effect on sales.

Fashion advertising divides into two main types:

- **Corporate advertising**
- **Product-based advertising**

Corporate advertising

Corporate advertising is generally part of a 'pull' strategy aimed at building up brand awareness and image; the advertising appeal is made to people's values, attitudes or lifestyle. Cecil Gee has used this type of advertising to good effect.

Product-based advertising

Product-based advertising is usually paid for jointly by the manufacturer and retailer. This type of advertising is aimed at giving product information and has far more rational appeal. Lycra by Du Pont and Gore-tex advertisements are probably the most well-known to the consumer.

THE ADVERTISING PROCESS

Advertising is either developed in-house or by an outside agency; the increasing internationalism of the fashion industry has led to a higher proportion of advertising being developed by the larger agencies.

Advertising agencies vary enormously in terms of their size and the type of work that they do. Some agencies concentrate on creative work, the so-called 'hot shops' and others focus on the less glamorous side of advertising such as media buying. Media buying is effectively buying space in newspapers, magazines and so on; the art is to maximize the number of target customers who will see the advertisement in relation to the amount of money spent on placing the advertisements. The agency will normally earn commission from the newpapers for the advertising space sold to clients.

The development of an advertising campaign consists of a series of steps, which can vary in actual detail from company to company. We list the eight key steps below:

1 **Identify target**　If effective communication is to take place, the target market must be fully understood. One feature of the fashion industry is the move away from broad segments towards increasingly narrowly defined targets.
2 **Define objectives**　The objective of an advertising campaign can be stated in quantifiable terms, such as the campaign's effect on sales volume. It can also be stated in communication terms, for example the creation of a particular image or product awareness.
3 **Decide campaign issues**　Which aspects of the company or product will be given prominence – the style, the value, the image are just some features that an advertising campaign can pick up on.
4 **Allocate budget**　Any further advertising decisions will be based on the amount available to spend. Budgets are usually allocated either by the marketing manager or the account director. The ideal budget-setting method is known as 'objective/task', where money is allocated according to what needs to be done to achieve the necessary objective.
5 **Media planning**　Media are selected which will ensure that the largest part of the target market will see the message.
6 **Creation of campaign**　Artwork and copy are used to create an appropriate message, either in the specialist or more general press.
7 **Implementation**　In the fashion industry the timing, which is crucial to the success of any advertising campaign, is even more crucial, since the seasons and social events must be brought into consideration.
8 **Control**　The whole process needs to be controlled to ensure that the right target is receiving the right message and acting upon it in terms of purchases. The usual control mechanisms applied to advertising

campaigns are feedback on sales, market research to test awareness and the budget as a means of retaining financial control.

ADVERTISING TOOLS AVAILABLE TO THE FASHION MARKETING MANAGER

There are many different ways to categorize advertising, the most commonly used categories are:

- **Above the line**   This covers media-based advertising (e.g. advertisements in magazines/stores)
- **Below the line**   This is non-media advertising (e.g. point-of-sale displays, especially for hosiery)

Above-the-line advertising uses seven major media to transmit its message:

- **Direct mail**
- **The press (newspapers and magazines)**
- **Posters**
- **Television**
- **Cinema**
- **Radio**
- **Minor media (e.g. taxis, video displays in public places, posters, etc.)**

We will consider each of these media in turn.

Direct mail

This really constitutes a stand-alone form of marketing. It is a useful medium for advertising, enabling potential customers to be pinpointed with enormous accuracy. It has been used to great effect by the Next Directory, for example.

The press

The press is becoming an increasingly popular medium for fashion advertising. The trade press has always carried a certain amount of advertising to business and specialist fashion magazines such as *Vogue* have always afforded the opportunity to target the required market. Now fashion advertisers are being more proactive, actually advertising in the non-fashion press to ensure targeting their key customers. Giorgio Armani targets affluent men in the 25–50 sector by advertising in *The Economist* for example.

Television

TV advertising is used for fashion items that rely on having a strong brand image, such as jeans and trainers, which do not appeal to a narrow market segment. In the 1960s, when undergarments such as bras and girdles were sold on product performance rather than style and brand image, television was a popular advertising medium for those products. Changes in the marketing strategy of these companies have moved advertisements from the television.

Cinema

Like television, cinema is used to create and reinforce brand image. The creators of the advertisements for Levis and Lee jeans began by creating a 'mini' film specifically for the cinema audience. They have almost created their own genre, with the Levi's 'launderette' advertisement probably being the most popular and successful.

Radio

Radio has not been a particularly useful medium for the fashion industry, an industry that relies heavily on visual images. However, the increasing popularity of commercial radio, and its relative cheapness, are making it a useful means of communicating information about retailer's sales and special offers. For example, in-store radio has also been used by 'Top Shop' as a medium for delivering information.

Posters

Billboards and posters have become an increasingly popular advertising medium for the fashion industry. They are an extremely cost-effective means of reinforcing a brand awareness campaign and can also create valuable publicity spin-offs, as shown by the notorious Benetton campaign. The main disadvantage of this medium is that it is almost impossible to target only one segment of the market.

Below-the-line advertising is closely allied to sales promotion, and is often used as a means of boosting sales in the short term. Below-the-line advertising falls into two categories:

- **consumer advertising**
- **business-to-business advertising**

Consumer advertising

Below-the-line advertising to the consumer is frequently aimed at producing a decision to purchase, such as:

- **Fashion shows organized by retailers**
- **Competitions organized by retailers**
- **Point-of-sale posters and leaflets giving further information about the product range**

Business-to-business

This type of advertising plays a very important role in fashion marketing due to the dominance of the fashion buyer in the whole marketing process. Typically, in the fashion industry, business-to-business advertising of this type includes:

- **Exhibitions, both national and international**
- **Merchandising support, Gossard offer display stands and posters to its stockists, for example**

Changes in advertising usage in the fashion industry have come about in recent years because of changes in the power of retailers, and a switch in marketing strategies towards greater segmentation of markets and concentration on image and brand awareness.

SALES PROMOTION

Sales promotion aims to increase sales by providing an extra motive for purchase or by encouraging retailers to stock particular items and market them. In the fashion industry, sales promotions fall into three major categories:

- **Promotions by sections of the industry as a whole**
- **promotions aimed at retailers**
- **Promotions targeted at consumers**

The key tools used by fashion marketers to promote both individual designers or companies and particular garments, include:

- **Displays**
- **Events**
- **Special features**
- **Fashion shows**
- **Packaging**
- **Multi-purpose promotions, e.g. store cards**

We will now examine how each of the sectors uses the promotions tools to assist their promotions strategy.

Industry/designer-based promotions

The British fashion industry has become more conscious of the need to promote itself at an international level and the main methods it has chosen have been special events and fashion shows. For example, a British Fashion Week was organized in Italy with the backing of the Department of Trade and Industry. This meant not only the conventional fashion shows and exhibitions, but backing in the form of receptions held for key buyers and other important figures in the industry.

The role of the British Fashion Council in promoting the British fashion industry both at home and abroad deserves particular mention. The British Fashion Council was formed in 1983 and since 1987 has received government funding and financial support from industrial sponsors which has enabled it to develop its central role in promoting the fashion industry. Its major activities are the organization of London Fashion Week, which acts as a magnet for the designer fashion industry, and also the British Fashion Awards, which provide an annual focus for the industry and receive wide coverage in the media.

The British Clothing Industry Association also plays an important role in promoting the fashion industry, through sponsorship of exhibitions and public relations programmes. At an international level, the British Knitting and Clothing Export Council organizes exhibitions and trade missions throughout the world which afford even the small companies the opportunity to exhibit at international level.

Fashion designers have also linked up with other organizations for promotional events, such as the link with Friends of the Earth, which produced the Rainforest Fashion Show. The show fulfilled the dual purpose of promoting new and exciting designs from established names like Edina Ronay and Vivienne Westwood and establishing the fashion industry's credentials as an environmentally aware industry.

The important feature about such industry-wide promotional activities is that they are not confined to one particular segment of the market such as retailers or a particular group of consumers. Most of these events aim to promote the importance of the industry as a whole and establish awareness of the fashion design industry.

Promotions aimed at retailers

Promotions aimed at retailers have a more specific purpose, that of encouraging them to stock a particular line or range of designs. Traditional methods, such as fashion shows aimed at buyers, such as the London Designer Show still hold sway. From a marketing perspective, this is a very 'product-orientated' approach, the designs being expected to 'sell themselves'. The changing economic scene is forcing fashion marketers to be more innovative in their approach, particularly in the assistance that they offer to retailers targeting different segments of the consumer market.

There still remains a difference in the way designs for garments are promoted compared to the way smaller fashion items such as tights are dealt with. The promotion of the smaller fashion item, which is sold through a greater variety of outlets, such as grocery chains, more closely resembles that used for other FMCG (fast-moving consumer goods), like chocolates. Promotional tools like discounting, together with provision of display stands and 'below-the-line' advertising materials are used more frequently.

Promotions targeted at the consumer

Traditionally, sales promotions aimed at the consumer were the domain of the retailer. The rise in importance of designer labels and brand image has extended the range of promotions, so that retailers frequently link up with manufacturers or designers for promotional events. Additionally, some fashion companies with a strong brand image are promoting direct to the consumer. The most widely used promotions to consumers are:

- **Price-based promotions**
- **Displays**
- **Features/events**
- **Consumer contests**
- **Trial offers**

- **Price-based promotions**   The most widely used price-based promotion in the fashion retailing industry is the sale, which offers substantial price reductions both to clear stock and to increase store traffic so that potential customers can see the new season's garments. Fashion marketers have become more innovative in their use of price-based promotions recently and have added price-off offers which give a small discount on a particular range for a limited time. This can boost short-term sales, but if used too frequently can dent a product's image.
- **Discounts**   The use of 'money-off coupons' or discounts has also gained ground in the fashion retail industry, although these are still used mainly by the larger organization, for example BhS gave discount stamps to customers spending over £10 in the store. When a certain number had been collected they entitled the customer to discounts, starting at 5 per cent, on future purchases.

- **Displays** Displays are a traditional method of promotion in the fashion retail industry. Again, they are product- rather than market-led. The two types of display most often used are the window display and the in-store display. The main purpose of such displays is to build up the store and product image; to be fully effective they need to be considered as part of the overall promotional strategy, reinforcing advertising and giving additional information about the product, such as price. The Liberty store in London is well known for the creative display of its goods both in the window and in-store.

- **Features and events** These are used by designers, manufacturers and fashion retailers to attract the consumer. The fashion show organized by the retailer remains a popular method of promotion; regular customers are invited to view the new seasons' garments at an invitation-only event. Increasingly, retailers are turning to special events as a method of promotion, for example 'Italian week', where not only food and other items, but also fashion is promoted linked to a particular theme.

- **Links with high-profile designers** These have also been used, particularly by mail order retailers to attract customers. A catalogue will carry one or two pages of designs either produced or endorsed by a well-known designer. The design team 'Workers for Freedom' (British Fashion Award winners) have produced collections for Brian Mills. This builds the image of the range carried as a whole and helps to increase turnover.

- **Fashion magazine promotions** Are becoming a widely used promotions tool which, again, demonstrate the move towards a less product-led strategy on the part of the fashion marketers. Fashion features within the magazine are produced jointly by the store and the magazine to feature particular new ranges. For example, in the April 1993 edition of Marie Claire the magazine contains a promotion with Selfridges called 'American Designers'.

    Mail order companies such as Janet Frazer also use fashion magazines for promotional features, for instance, the inclusion of several pages of clothes selected by the fashion editor of *19*. This type of feature allows the fashion marketer to target the consumer more accurately and to emphasize product benefits of direct relevance to their target consumer.

    Consumer contests are not frequently used in the fashion retail industry; this is where consumers compete for prizes based upon a competition requiring some analytical skill. They are occasionally used by some of the larger retailers. Consumer sweepstakes, e.g. Next Directory prize draw, where consumers are entered into a prize draw if they purchase a particular item, can be used as a means of boosting sales in the short term.

- **Trial offers**   These are used by designers as a means of attracting new customers and stimulating word-of-mouth advertising. Trial offers in the fashion industry can rarely consist of free samples (except for hosiery) although some designers do allow high profile customers to wear their designs in order to promote press coverage and word-of-mouth advertising. Many designers will offer a garment at substantially reduced prices via exclusive offers in fashion magazines (e.g. March 1993 edition of *Elle* features as its special offer a shirt by Nicholas Knightly), this helps stimulate product usage and promote brand image.

    The drawback with all consumer promotions is that they can only stimulate sales in the short term. If carried on for too long, or in too great a quantity, they can begin to have a damaging effect on the company's image. This is partly because they tend to be used when a product has already been adopted by trendsetters or is going into its decline phase.

Occasionally the promotions are not aimed directly at the consumer but at the sales staff. Pepe, in line with other jeans manufacturers, has launched sales staff incentive schemes to encourage staff loyalty to the label. One scheme gives staff a point for every pair of Pepe jeans sold. When the member of staff reaches 250 points they are entitled to enter a draw for a car.

PUBLICITY

Publicity is concerned with communicating with the market via news stories or features. The editorial space is not paid for and thus carries more authority than a paid advertisement.

In some industries, publicity is a minor part of overall marketing activities, in others publicity forms part of the entirely separate activity of public relations; so it is with the fashion industry, where public relations is an important activity in its own right. With such a short time-cycle to operate in and in such a high-risk business, intensive exposure to the media is vital for success. The immense high profile of Fashion PR 'giants' such as Lynne Franks testifies to this powerful role.

The marketing manager needs to work closely with the public relations department to ensure that they are pursuing common goals and that publicity harmonizes with the other promotional activities of the company. Publicity has the benefit of carrying an aura of independence because it is information from a third party and not paid-for advertising. For the fashion marketer, it has the advantage that a huge audience for the message can be obtained for a fraction of the price of paid advertising. A picture of the clothes of a particular designer on the back of an internationally famous person like Princess Diana can create enormous attention.

The problem for the fashion marketer with publicity is that it is no longer within the department's control, parts of the message may be deleted or the content altered to fit in with the editor's own requirements. In addition, with broadcast media the message can appear at times suitable for the media, and these are not necessarily the times when it will achieve maximum exposure to the fashion marketer's target audience. Negative publicity is also very powerful and something which fashion marketers need to plan for. Stories about poor-quality products or photographs of unsuccessful designs can haunt a marketer for several seasons afterwards. The speed with which publicity operates makes it important that public relations are placed on a firm footing within the organization.

PERSONAL SELLING

The role of personal selling in fashion marketing

Some types of fashion retailing do not require extensive use of sales personnel. Larger fashion retailers which operate an essentially self-service approach, such as Marks and Spencer, are an example. The trend towards mail order shopping has also diminished the importance of personal selling as a component of the promotions mix for many organizations. However, personal selling still plays a key role in more exclusive outlets like Joseph and Browns, it is also important in department stores where concessions such as Jaques Vert, Planet and Mondi have their own sales personnel.

The key role of the sales person is to inform customers about the product and to influence the decision to buy. The role of the sales person is crucial, because they represent the company to the consumer. As successful personal selling relies on building a positive relationship between consumer and sales person, sales people are also in a key position to give feedback to the marketing manager on the consumers' response to particular lines.

Relationship between the marketing manager and sales personnel

Personal selling, like publicity, is an area of the promotions mix where the fashion marketing manager needs to co-operate closely with other functions within the business. In this case s/he needs to work with the personnel department (in the case of large organizations such as Acquascutum) to ensure that customers' needs are met.

Careful selection and training of sales people is especially important for the fashion company. Sales personnel need to reflect the right image, their own style should match that of the company and their approach to customers should be appropriate to the target market. This is where the fashion company relies on good co-operation between the personnel and marketing functions.

In order to ensure that sales personnel are fully informed about the latest developments in the company, the marketing manager should ideally develop an 'internal marketing programme' in addition to training offered by the human resources/personnel department. Internal marketing aims at raising interest and awareness of the fashion range, as well as developing product knowledge. Typical internal marketing tools for communicating with sales personnel include:

- **Fashion shows**
- **Discounts**
- **Videos**
- **Briefings**

These encourage a lively interest in fashion which is important if the sales person is to market the range effectively and enthusiastically to customers.

The personal selling process

As with the other elements in the fashion promotions mix, personal selling aims to communicate with customers, to inform them and persuade them to buy. The actual sales process can be broken down into the following stages:

- **Approach/relationship formation**
- **Inform/discuss**
- **Demonstrate/feedback**
- **Close sale**
- **Packaging**

Buying fashion items is known in marketing terms as a 'high involvement' process. Although the decision-making process remains basically the same whatever item is being bought, far more of the customer's identity is at stake when they buy a fashion item than when they buy a more expensive, but nevertheless emotionally neutral product such as a freezer. In fashion purchases, emotional involvement is high. In addition, because fashion items are highly differentiated, unlike traditional 'low involvement' items such as confectionary bars, the level of rational decision making involved in the purchase is also high.

The approach/relationship formation is a key stage in the fashion selling process. The sales person needs to gain the trust of the prospective customer, so that the customer is willing to accept advice and suggestions.

The next step in the process is to inform/discuss the purchase; the sales person needs to establish what the consumer's needs are, for instance, is the garment needed for a special occasion or for business wear? They are then in a position to inform the customer about the range of choices available, give further details about pricing and availability of additional items to complement the outfit.

The sales person will then show garments to the customer, demonstrating particular design features, possibly referring to additional promotion material. If the customer wishes to try a garment, the sales person should give tactful and helpful feedback, this is especially important if the customer is shopping alone. This is a particularly sensitive part of the sales process; what the sales person is often dealing with is the customer's self-image, they are not just selling a fashion item, but an element of the customer's own image.

This crucial stage of the selling process differentiates the marketing-orientated fashion sales person from the purely product- and profit-led personnel. The product-led sales person will be more concerned with the appeal of the garment itself, and will not be sensitive to how the customer feels about it; the profit-led sales person will be concerned with pressing for a sales close regardless of how satisfied the customer is with the product. The marketing-orientated sales force is aware of the fact that the customer must live with their purchase decision and that it is a vital part of the wearer's personal expression. A large amount of post-purchase dissatisfaction caused by buying the wrong garment under pressure will not only ensure that the customer is reluctant to return, but will also generate negative word-of-mouth advertising.

The close of the sale is when the sales person helps the consumer to reach the actual decision to purchase. In actual terms, this will mean that the sales person then takes the garment to the cash desk and instigates the payment process. At this point, if the purchase decision is very definite, the sales assistant may offer supplementary purchases, such as a small fashion item like a scarf.

Packing is a particularly important finishing touch to the sales process, having the garment carefully packed adds a service dimension to the purchase process. Even essentially self-service fashion stores such as Jigsaw will pay attention to careful packing of the garment.

Managing the sales force is an important activity, sales people represent the company, and also generate a high proportion of turnover and profit. Deciding how to pay sales people is a further consideration of the marketing manager, as method of payment can impact heavily on sales performance and the type of sales transactions that take place. Although paying a substantial part of the salary in the form of commission can have a short-term positive impact on sales, the tendency to 'push' garments, thus reducing long-term sales is a danger. That is why calculating a marketing orientation in the sales force is so important.

SUMMARY

In fashion marketing the four promotional mix elements:

- **Advertising**
- **Sales promotions**
- **Publicity**
- **Personnel selling**

are used slightly differently to mainstream consumer marketing. The promotions effort requires strong co-operation between designers, manufacturers and the distribution channels.

Changes in the way that fashion has been marketed in recent years have given the fashion marketer a wider range of tools with which to develop promotions strategies. As with any successful marketing effort, it also requires strong co-operation with other functions within the business.

DISCUSSION POINTS

1 Design an advertising campaign for a well-known company, outline the stages that will take place.
2 A multiple retail chain wishes to promote a more individual look in each of its shops. What strategies would you advise to ensure that local shoppers understand the message?
3 There are many industry/designer based promotions. Select one type of product (e.g. swimwear) and research into the possible ways that it could be promoted.
4 A company is relaunching an old 'classic'. Research a garment that was fashionable years ago (such as a mohair suit of the 1960s) and design a press conference for the company's promotion of the garment. Design the press pack that you would have available.

Chapter 10

Fashion public relations

THE IMPORTANCE OF FASHION PUBLIC RELATIONS

Fashion public relations is probably the most glamorous and high-profile fashion marketing activity. The best known fashion public relations specialist, Lynne Franks, is easily as famous as some of the designers she helps to promote. Indeed, fashion marketing can appear to be over-shadowed by fashion PR, simply because it has such an image. In reality, fashion PR should help to support the whole marketing effort, and draw on research carried out by the marketing department to increase its effectiveness.

In this chapter, we will start by reaching an understanding of what we mean by the term 'fashion public relations'. Then we will look at the fashion PR industry in the UK, and how it relates to the fashion industry as a whole. We look at the major fashion public relations activities of the manager, and examine the main tools s/he will use in carrying out this job. Finally, we examine the role of fashion public relations in the overall fashion marketing effort.

What do we understand by the term fashion public relations? Firstly, it is important to draw the distinction between fashion marketing and fashion public relations. Fashion marketing is primarily concerned with satisfying the customers' needs, wants and demands, and ensuring that the fashion organization meets them (see Chapter 1). Fashion marketing, even in those sectors of the industry that are primarily designer-led, will include a whole range of activities such as distribution management and pricing strategy. The primary concern of fashion public relations is with communications, which can be targeted at groups other than just the company's customers.

The Institute of Public Relations defines PR as the 'deliberate, planned and sustained effort to establish and maintain a mutual understanding between an organization and its public.' Although we tend only to become aware of the work of the fashion PR specialist at the time of an 'event' like a fashion show, most of the work that is carried out takes place throughout the year and is indeed a sustained effort. The communication is not limited to specifics like the launch of a new set of designs, nor is it a haphazard response to an event, such as an adverse response to a series of advertisements, but an ongoing activity.

The emphasis on mutual understanding is an important aspect of fashion public relations. Just look at how one of the major tasks for the public relations consultants of the main fashion industry bodies has been to convince key decision makers in government and finance of the importance of the fashion industry to the country's economy.

As far as fashion public relations is concerned, the organization could be just one designer or a major listed company like Laura Ashley. The concept of the 'public' of a fashion company is particularly complex, and it is important to point out that the public for a high-fashion designer such as Arabella Pollen will be vastly different from that of a mainsteam fashion retailer like Dorothy Perkins.

If we look at the vast range of 'publics' a top designer like Vivienne Westwood is addressing, it gives us some idea of the scope of the fashion public relations task. When Vivienne Westwood's autumn 1993 collection was launched, the public did not only consist of those who might buy her designs, there was an 'inner circle' of fellow top designers, like Jean Paul Gaultier and Azzedine Alaia, and 'supermodels' to consider as a starting point; ecstatic comments from fellow designers and the news that supermodels are prepared to work without fees for the chance of owning the clothes can generate useful publicity in itself. The next 'line' that needed to be addressed was the fashion journalists from the national and international press, who would disseminate news and photographs about the new collection throughout the world. Also important on this level were the buyers of the large exclusive stores, such as Liberty of London which now sells Westwood wedding dresses. A further segment of the 'public' for Westwood's Autumn collection were representatives of firms in the fashion industry looking to capitalize on the Westwood name to market their own products, for example Swatch, the watch company, or Littlewoods, whose summer 1994 catalogue will contain a Westwood collection. Those who buy her clothes will be reached largely through the work of the fashion journalists, who will be targeted carefully and given assistance to produce copy which will effectively put across the Westwood message.

Nor will the PR effort be limited to those in the world of fashion; financial backers will also need the reassurance of future success that can be given by effective handling of public relations highlighted by an event such as a fashion show.

THE FASHION PR INDUSTRY IN THE UK

Fashion PR plays an increasingly important role in the marketing of fashion. It is significant that fashion companies are adopting a more structured approach to their communications and this is reflected in the development of this aspect of the industry in the UK. In this section we will take an overview of the size and character of the industry, including a look at its major players. We will also look at the range of its activities and see how approaches to PR differ in the UK to other EC countries.

The fashion public relations industry has grown enormously over the past decade. *Fashion Monitor*, which is fast becoming the Fashion Public Relations 'bible' holds over 160 PR companies with listed fashion accounts. While many of the companies included, such as Good Relations and Shandwick, are large films covering a range of industries, specialist fashion public relations firms are an established feature of the industry and well over half the firms listed specialize in fashion PR alone.

No discussion of UK fashion PR can omit to mention Lynne Franks, who helped to establish fashion PR as an industry in its own right. She does not dominate the industry in terms of numbers of clients, rather in terms of their turnover (she has the account for Laura Ashley for example), their prestige (Jean Paul Gaultier is another client) and their power within the industry (she handles PR for the British Fashion Council). She has the highest relative market share of all the industry body accounts.

Now, specialist fashion PR firms dominate the market in certain sectors, for example designers tend to prefer fashion specialists, and in this market, Jean Bennet who holds Jeff Banks' account has the largest relative market share. Even firms with their own in-house PR offices may find fashion PR firms are frequently used for large 'set piece' events such as fashion shows, or product launches.

Despite the large amount of expertise available, many designers continue to handle their PR in-house. Indeed, nearly 50 per cent of designers listed by *Fashion Monitor* have their own in-house PR offices, including famous names like Giorgio Armani and Katharine Hamnett. Large retailers also vary in their approach to PR; Marks and Spencer handle their own in-house, whereas Burberry uses the Stephanie Churchill agency.

Although PR agencies are useful for organizing special occasions and for developing relations with the press, there are also occasions when everyone within the fashion company will need to be able to deal with publicity. Some designers, such as Elizabeth Emanuel, actually retain responsibility for their own PR all the time.

It is important to note that many parts of the UK fashion industry will actually have different PR needs because they are addressing different publics. An industry body such as the Fashion Council will speak to a wide audience which includes industrialists, legislators and financiers; retailers will need to speak more directly to the end consumer; and designers to both their elite customers who actually buy the designs and to the manufacturers interested in making goods under licence with the designer's name. There is a great diversity of communications channels reflecting the diverse publics the industry needs to address. The UK has over 65 magazines which carry fashion features and articles ranging from *Cosmopolitan* and *GQ* to *Best* and *Jackie*. Newspapers also carry fashion articles from the *Sun* to the *Independent*, and there are over 50 local and regional papers which carry fashion items. All of them present a means of communicating with the end consumer, and enable the PR company or office to target the appropriate market, be it geographical in the case of a retailer, or demographic, as in the case of a label.

In addition to promoting direct to the consumer, there is also the possibility of targeting buyers through the trade press; over 20 titles exist which cater for various aspects of the fashion industry in the UK, some of them very specifically targeted, such as *Bridal Buyer*. So the fashion PR specialist can either target the buyers or the end customers of the merchandise which s/he is promoting.

The key difference between fashion PR in the UK and in the EC lies in targeting. In Chapter 4 we have already pointed out that the UK differs somewhat from other EC countries in that it is dominated by the multiple chains. This contrast also extends into the way in which fashion PR is handled in the UK.

The launch of 'Soviet' brand jeans amply illustrates the issue. When the jeans were launched in Italy and France, the launch partly took place direct to the trade in railway stations redolent of *Anna Karenina* and *Dr Zhivago*, the PR agency tried to get across the image that these jeans had arrived straight from Russia. It was important to promote the jeans to the industry as a whole. In the UK, the product was launched in a completely different way, the distribution network for the jeans was quietly built up, then the jeans were promoted directly to the consumer. This totally different approach to PR stems from an entirely different approach to marketing. The importance of the distribution networks in the UK is worth noting. The big retail chains carry out a great deal of fashion public relations both on their own account and in conjunction with the designers they stock. In other parts of Europe, where fashion distribution is dominated by smaller shops, it is more important to target the trade than the consumer.

HOW IS FASHION PR MANAGED?

As we have pointed out, fashion companies can vary considerably in the way in which they organize their public relations. Some names, like

Silhouette, will use a large full-service agency like McCann, whose McCann PR is part of a wider advertising agency; others will use a specialist fashion PR agency. The choices open to a fashion company, be they designer, manufacturer or retailer are:

- **In-house PR**
- **Freelance PR specialist**
- **Specialist fashion PR agency**
- **Full-service advertising agency**
- **Non-specialist PR firm**

In-house PR remains a popular choice with many firms and offers some advantages in that someone is always on call to deal with press enquiries and to liaise with journalists needing to borrow stock for photo shoots and so on. In some organizations the PR department operates independently, but in many of the larger organizations it is part of overall marketing activities.

The drawback with in-house PR is that sometimes the resources might not be available to deal with a really large event. Many firms opt for a freelance PR specialist who often has several clients on his/her list. In this way the company has access to the necessary expertise when it is needed and does not have the expense of maintaining an office all the time.

The specialist fashion PR agency offers the advantage of well-developed contacts with the trade press and with the fashion editors of the important magazines and daily newspapers. They also have a concentration of expertise on industry-specific PR tasks such as organizing fashion shows.

A full-service agency offers the advantage of being able to tie in PR with other promotional activity, it also has a wide range of research facilities to draw on. Another aspect which is important for the larger firm is the access that these agencies may be able to obtain for other interest groups, for example shareholders and financiers.

Whichever approach the fashion company decides to take to PR, the PR manager or fashion account executive will carry out the same basic activities:

- **Press relations**
- **Publicity material and resources**
- **Corporate communications**
- **Fashion events**

We will discuss each of these activities and the tasks involved in turn.

Press relations

As the Institute of Public Relations' definition of PR implies, developing and maintaining good relations with the press is one of the key PR activities. This needs to be done throughout the year, not just when there is a key product launch. Two characteristics of the fashion industry make press relations a particularly important activity: one is the very short product life cycles and restricted seasons within the fashion industry, the other is the high level of competition. In the fast-changing world of fashion, those organizations who do not put in sustained effort in cultivating press relations lose out to those who do.

The basic tasks that need to be carried out by the fashion public relations manager are as follows:

- **Information** Journalists and editors must be kept informed of all developments in the company. This is usually done by keeping an up-to-date mailing list and most fashion PR managers will use *Fashion Monitor* to update their lists.
- **Contacts** Good personal relationships must be maintained by keeping social contact with key fashion editors. For example, many of the larger companies will hold regular lunches for important journalists who thus have the opportunity to get close to the organization.
- **Service** PR agencies and in-house offices will also ensure that they run an efficient service for journalists who may require garments for photo shoots and interviews with designers.
- **Publicity** PR agencies will also work at producing publicity material (which is discussed below), for example, co-ordinating stylists, models and photographers for photographs or videos of new designs.

These are just some of the activities that the fashion PR office will do to ensure that a journalist will write about their particular range rather than a rival's. It requires careful selection of the target editors, for example, the retailers Etam would target editors of young fashion magazines like *Just Seventeen*, rather than *Vogue* or *Marie Claire*. Effective press relations are a necessary background to all the other fashion PR activities listed above, at the same time, all of the other activities contribute to effective management of communications between the fashion company and its publics.

Publicity material and resources

Fashion public relations involves not only cultivating goodwill among those who can communicate the latest company developments, it also involves triggering action. This is done by production of publicity material and resources aimed at the media with the intention that they will then use it to produce news stories, features and editorials. A variety of techniques are open to the fashion PR office. Those most frequently used are:

- Press release
- Captioned photographs
- Organization of personal interviews
- Press conference/press launch

We will discuss each of the techniques below:

- **Press releases**   These are some of the most frequently used PR tools. They usually consist of one A4-sized sheet containing brief details of a 'newsworthy' item, such as the launch of a new collection by a designer, together with contact names and numbers of the fashion PR account director or in-house manager. These are circulated to all editors who might have an interest in publishing the story.

  The problems for the fashion PR office are twofold. First, the editor may alter the emphasis of the story in some way, by excluding some of the information in the original press release since the PR office no longer has any control over the material once it has been released. Second, the press release is such a commonly used form of publicity material that it has to compete with a myriad of other press releases from other firms. This is where the sustained cultivation of journalists pays off, since they are more likely to notice a press release put out by a familiar company.

- **Captioned photographs**   Captioned photographs are used in conjunction with the press release to secure editorial space. These are photographs taken by the PR office's own selected photographers and released to the media. While the major newspapers and magazines will usually have their own photographers who will follow up big stories, the lower budget fashion pages and some parts of the trade press are able to make good use of such material.

- **Organized personal interviews**   Specially organized interviews are also part of the PR specialist's stock in trade. Arranging for journalists from radio and television as well as the fashion pages to interview a leading designer like Paul Smith following the launch of a new collection or the opening of a new shop is a mutually beneficial exercise. On such occasions, there may be many journalists seeking interviews, and it is the PR specialists' job to know which interviews are most likely to be read, seen or heard by the key target markets.

- **Press conferences/launches**   Press events are another frequently used techniques for generating press interest and coverage of important issues. The British Fashion Council has successfully used the press conference as a device to gain media attention for their campaign to get more government support for the fashion industry. An important feature of the press conference is that it gives the opportunity for two-way communication; the press is able to put questions to key individuals, e.g. the chairperson, who can answer them on the spot.

Press launches for new collections tend to be far more 'glossy' affairs, often held in interesting venues to tempt weary journalists to attend. The launch of the first Principles shop actually took place in the store, where journalists had the opportunity to see the merchandise and the layout first hand, as well as to sample the ample refreshments that were on hand! At this type of event, the fashion public relations specialist will ensure that each journalist is supplied with a 'press pack' which contains a much longer version of the press release together with photographs, promotional literature and corporate gifts, all of which help to create a positive image in the hope of gaining more coverage for the story.

Corporate communications

One of the key features of fashion public relations is that communication is planned, it does not take place on an *ad hoc* basis. This extends to both published and personal communications. An effective Fashion PR specialist will ensure that all corporate communications help to fulfil the purpose of fostering good communications. Therefore, corporate publications like the Laura Ashley *Annual Report* and *Accounts* are seen as not only a financial document, but also as a PR document, which must have a stylish design in keeping with the company's corporate image. Similarly, by assisting in the production of educational material, as did the Burton group, who featured in some of the Open University's Business Studies courses, for instance, the company is able to put its message across to a very specific audience.

Personal communication also plays an important part in the overall communications effort. The form that this communication takes depends largely on the organization involved. The PR representatives of an industry body like the BCIA will be involved in lobbying interest groups, for example environmentalists who may feel that the clothing industry, through its use of chemicals and dyes is environmentally destructive. The task of a PR specialist employed by a big-name designer will be to counsel them on how to respond to interviews and to offer advice on TV appearances and techniques.

Fashion events

The fashion event most closely associated with the fashion PR industry is the large scale fashion show of big-name designers such as Jasper Conran. These will be widely reported in the powerful fashion pages of the daily papers, and in television news. Fashion shows have grown from being promotional events into artistic creations in themselves, with fashion show videos now on sale to the public.

However, in addition to these seasonal events, there are a whole range of other fashion events that can be used to promote designers or new ranges:

- **In-store exhibitions**   These events are used to promote designers or labels from a particular part of Europe, for example. These are focused directly on the consumer market, though some of them do attract a certain amount of media attention, particularly popular and successful are those held in exclusive stores like Liberty.
- **Public exhibitions**   This approach is increasingly popular as a means of getting in contact with the target markets. The largest exhibitions of this type are the 'Clothes Show Live' events.
- **Trade exhibitions**   These are the other main fashion events used by the PR specialist for promotion purposes. Events like the Harrogate Eveningwear Exhibition allow manufacturers and designers to make contact with the buyers, but skilful PR management can ensure that promotional literature and well-trained staff on hand increase the company's success.
- **Charity events**   Charity fund-raising events are used increasingly to demonstrate that the fashion industry is not entirely hedonistic and uncaring. Charity balls offer the opportunity for garments to be seen on the backs of the rich and famous. Charity fashion shows, to raise money for causes like AIDS research, also aim to demonstrate a socially responsible aspect of the industry. These various activities and techniques will be used by the fashion public relations office to secure particular objectives by using the appropriate communications technique targeted at the right market.

THE ROLE OF FASHION PUBLIC RELATIONS IN THE TOTAL FASHION MARKETING EFFORT

If a company plans its marketing activities adequately, then it goes without saying that fashion PR will play an important role in promoting the fashion company and in supporting initiatives such as changes in distribution strategy. Sometimes fashion public relations works as a separate part of the company's activities, which has its dangers, because the communications can get out of step with events taking place in the rest of the company. Publicity complements other paid forms of communication; for example, Levi jeans advertisements are always preceded by press coverage gained, ensuring that viewers will pay more attention to them. Fashion PR is also needed to build up longer-term relationships with the public and with the media who inform them. Good PR will not just be one-way communication, but will help to ensure that the company is aware of how the consumer feels about the company.

Fashion PR must work closely with the rest of the marketing team if it is to have an impact on sales and profits and this partnership will mean that the PR office then has access not only to the items which can help to create the news but to the information needed to target it accurately.

SUMMARY

In this chapter, we have:

- Defined fashion public relations as ongoing planned communications activity, the aim of which is to foster understanding and two-way communication between the fashion organization and its publics.
- Examined the structure and specialist nature of the UK fashion industry.
- Discussed the various ways in which fashion companies can organize their PR activities: in-house, freelance specialist, specialist agency, full service ad agency, multi-client PR firm.
- Examined the activities of the PR specialist: press relations, publicity material and resources, corporate communications and fashion events.
- Looked at the role of fashion PR in the total marketing effort.

DISCUSSION POINTS

1 You work as a freelance PR for a designer who has just produced a new range of sportswear. Outline the main PR activities which you would organize for your client.
2 Select a major 'name' in the fashion world and find examples of their publicity material. Evaluate them in terms of their effectiveness, communication and reflection of fashion image.
3 PR can be of major importance to the company when things go wrong. Select an example of how a company has handled negative publicity and discuss any alternative courses of action that could be taken.

Chapter 11

Marketing planning for the fashion industry

THE NEED FOR THE FASHION MARKETER TO EMPLOY PLANNING

For many people, marketing planning is synonymous with US industrial giants. It can seem out of place in the changing, design-orientated world of fashion. As always, appearances can be deceptive.

The era of the 'fashion dictator' has long passed (Evans 1989). Consumers are ever more informed and sophisticated in their response and the competitive environment is fiercer than ever. Marketing planning allows those working in all areas of the fashion industry to gain some measure of control and understanding over the different factors which work to create their marketplace, and to ensure that their organization marshals its resources effectively to meet those challenges.

Marketing planning is useful both to the designer, who needs to understand the context in which s/he works, particularly if they decide to link up with one of the larger clothing or textile manufacturers as Vivienne Westwood has done with Coats Viyella. It is also imperative for the marketing manager of the small- to medium-sized enterprise to take on board marketing planning concepts if they are to compete effectively in a rapidly changing business environment.

WHAT IS FASHION MARKETING PLANNING ALL ABOUT?

All marketing plans, no matter how they are developed or what the industrial context, will have certain common factors. The marketing plan will set out how the organization will use the means at its disposal to achieve its marketing objectives or goals. For example, many fashion companies, notably German manufactures, aim to achieve dominance of a particular market segment by creating a strong brand image. The marketing plan will harness diverse issues like the product, quality and design, communications strategy, distribution strategy and pricing policy to ensure the objective is achieved.

Depending on the character of the company the marketing process can be either formal or informal. In other words, a set of systems can be put in place to gather and interpret data, or the plan can be organized informally by senior management. The marketing plan should not be driven by the internal needs of the company, but should harmonize those internal needs with the demands and constraints of the business environment.

The ultimate goal of the marketing plan should be to ensure that customer satisfaction is maximized.

Approaches to marketing planning have changed over the last decade. In many ways, marketing managers in other industries are now having to deal with a range of problems that have always confronted the fashion marketing manager, such as rapid rate of change and vulnerability to the business environment. Although the framework of the marketing plan remains the same, it is important for the fashion marketer to realize that the document should not be regarded as set in tablets of stone, but recognized as a guideline from which it is possible to make sensible deviations.

Fashion marketers must not only adhere to the same principles as other marketers, they also need to take on board those factors that are unique to the fashion industry (Hook 1987). In their external environment, they must work in a highly competitive industry that is subject to change both through the seasons and the product life cycle (see Chapter 5), and deal with a consumer who is motivated by inner psychological factors to a much greater degree than, say, the consumer of a washing machine.

Before we go on to explain the various factors which need to be taken into account, it is important to have a picture of the basic planning process. This is presented in Figure 11.1.

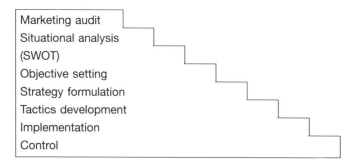

Marketing audit
Situational analysis
(SWOT)
Objective setting
Strategy formulation
Tactics development
Implementation
Control

Figure 11.1 Marketing planning – the basic process

The various aspects of Figure 11.1 are explained below:

- **Marketing audit**   In this, the information-gathering stage of the process, factors such as the macro-environment, micro-environment, marketing mix and management of the company must be taken into account.
- **Situational analysis**   This stage, sometimes known as the 'SWOT', short for Strengths, Weaknesses, Opportunities and Threats, is where the information is sorted and evaluated.
- **Objective setting**   At this stage the marketer decides what the organization's current goals are (e.g. to increase market share or profits).
- **Strategy formulation**   Once objectives have been set the organization can now begin to decide how it will achieve its objectives, usually by developing the marketing mix to suit new products or markets.
- **Tactics development**   This stage concerns the detailed issues of the plan, such as media selection for promotions.
- Implementation   The plan will be implemented over a period of time, this is the stage at which the plan is activated.
- **Control**   Control is the means by which the plan is monitored, it ensures that budgets are being adhered to, and planned targets are being met.

All of these issues will be examined in much greater depth later in this chapter, but it is important to have a general idea of the planning process in order to appreciate the picture of fashion marketing that will be unfolded in the next sections.

KEY FACTORS INVOLVED IN FASHION MARKETING PLANNING

From the start, we have explained that marketing planning cannot take place in a vacuum, the key driving forces for change both from the company and consumer perspective come from the business environment. Understanding the marketing environment is not an optional extra for fashion marketers; it both sets the tone of the plan and determines its success or failure. In the introductory chapter of the book, we examined the impact of the environment on the fashion marketing effort as a whole. Here, we will single out the factors which influence the development of the marketing plan, and evaluate them. These key factors are:

- International nature of the fashion industry
- Politics and government
- Economics
- Social

- Technological
- Ecological environment
- Legal

Each of these factors is evaluated below:

- **International nature of the fashion industry**   Although the issue of fashion marketing in an international context is dealt with more fully elsewhere in this book, here we need to consider its impact on the planning process. The international context in which the fashion marketing plan will be developed has several important consequences:
  - **Internal nature of competition**
  - **Market segmentation**   will it be national or cross-national?
  - **Product development**   will products be developed for national or international markets?
  - **Distribution**   what forms will our distribution channels take?

- **Politics**   The attitude of government to a particular industry is crucial to its success, both in specific terms and in relation to buisness as a whole. The French government has long supported its indigenous fashion industry, both in terms of the promotion it gives to French designers and the facilities it allows the fashion industry, for example the huge exhibition space at the Pompidou Centre. The British government has begun to take a more proactive stance towards the fashion industry, which certainly places more resources in the hands of UK-based fashion marketers. Not only does it fully support the work of the Fashion Council (government ministers have been present at many of their exhibitions), but the Department of Trade and Industry is also able to assist marketing managers wishing to break into overseas fashion markets.

- **Economics**   In fashion marketing, economics has a twofold effect. First, there is the impact on fashion itself, as we have discussed elsewhere in the book; and second, there is the effect on the underlying business structure. In developing a marketing plan, the fashion marketer must be aware of issues like changes in exchange rates affecting prices, as well as the impact of the economic cycle on consumer spending.

- **Social factors**   Like economics, social factors will have a similar twofold impact on fashion marketing plans. Fashion itself is a social process which is highly responsive to social change and trends. In developing a marketing plan, the marketing manager must be sensitive both to the demographic issues that will directly affect the size of their market (for example, the huge rise in the numbers of working mothers has led to the development of fashion maternity wear) and also to social attitudes themselves which will affect marketing strategy, for instance French Connection is now positioning itself as a socially responsible company.

- **Ecological/environmental factors**   These factors play a crucial role in social attitudes as well as more practical concerns about the impact of the fashion industry on the environment. The industry itself is often accused of having a negative effect on the environment, with pollution from delivery vehicles and textile factories amongst the key problems. The marketing planner needs to take account of these issues. Fashion marketers tend to tackle these issues on two fronts, by using promotions to position themselves as environmentally responsible, and also by investigating how they can change aspects of their marketing mix to accommodate environmental issues. For example, along with developing household products that are kinder to the environment, Tesco's sells the Green Goods clothing range designed by Jeff Banks.
- **Legal factors**   No marketing planner can afford to ignore the law. S/he must ensure that products manufactured by the organization conform to legal standards and that promotions and pricing are also within the law.

These factors together can be described as the macro-environment, they are factors that will affect all companies within the industry, their impact varying only in the detail of its effect. The micro-environmental factors are those which are specific to the particular fashion company that we are concerned with. These will exercise a more direct influence over the types of strategy and plans which will develop. The major micro-environmental factors are now examined.

Competitive environment

The international character of the fashion industry is reflected in the competitive environment. Competition is not only from within the EC but from all over the globe. Supplies of raw materials (e.g. cotton) frequently come from abroad, and profitability is often dependent on export sales, to the US and Japan, for instance.

Corporate mission/strategy

The fashion marketer needs to work within the overall context of the organization's corporate strategy. While this is not an important issue for the small, informal organization, for large multinational producers and retailers it is. For example, the overall strategy of the organization may be to maximize the return on capital invested in the short term. This is frequently the case when the company is a subsidiary or is owned by an investment company. Thus, the corporate plan may create limits for the fashion marketer, who may have longer-term goals for market penetration. In the late 1980s the creation of the Storehouse group, with its vision of a synergistic group of companies dominated by a design ethos created many constraints for fashion marketers within the group.

Consumerism

Although the consumer movement as a whole affects marketing planning, specific issues have a direct bearing on fashion marketing planning. One particular example would be the ethical dilemmas raised by brand-name power in the teenage market. In the early 1990s, the National Consumer Council in the UK has been at the forefront of raising questions about strategy of high brand awareness adopted by manufacturers of fashion trainers. The National Consumer Council was concerned that this was putting the young consumer under unnecessary social strain. Any marketing plan, particularly in a socially sensitive field like fashion, needs to be beware of impact on the consumer and possible backlash, any strategy might have.

Stakeholders

We have already discussed the issue of corporate strategy and the fashion marketer. There is also the concern of stakeholders in the company, for example shareholders and investment companies. The marketing plan needs to take into account their needs. Whereas a family-run business may be content just to earn enough profits to survive, one owned by an investment company would be expected to maximize return on capital. Sometimes this can lead to a conflict of interest. This was the case with the Scottish clothing manufacturer MacBean. Although management wanted to diversify the product range and to improve product quality believing the market was ripe for these changes, the investment company that owned it was unwilling to invest large sums of money in the company and wanted, for example, to buy second-hand equipment rather than investing in up-to-date equipment that would provide quality finishes. In this particular case, the tension between the desire to satisfy the market and the stakeholders' interests proved too much, and the result was a management buyout.

WHAT ARE THE MAIN APPROACHES TO MARKETING PLANNING?

Although the outcome of the marketing process, the marketing plan, is important, the process iself plays a key role in business success. The planning process forces the organization or individual in the fashion industry to look outside the arena of the design, production or retail task, and to consider the broader issues which will affect the business in both long and short term.

Various approaches to planning can be taken, there is no 'right' or 'wrong' approach. Some of the most frequently used methods will be discussed here, as will the following key issues of:

- **Information flows**: top-down or bottom-up?
- **The planning cycle**
- **Crisis management**
- **New approaches to planning**

Information flows: the 'top-down' approach

In some larger organizations, marketing planning is an activity which takes place among the upper ranks of management, on the basis of ideas or information available to them. Implementation is the next stage, and the ideas are then 'pushed' downward through the organization. The process is essentially a tidy one, following decisions to be made and acted upon quickly. It can also mean, however, that the top managers become blinded by their own ideas and fail to notice changes in the environment or problems within their own organization which could hamper the progress of these ideas. To some extent, this 'top-down' approach contributed to Next's problems in the late 1980s. Under George Davies' leadership, the company began expanding in all directions – jewellery, gardening, and so on, without sufficient feedback from those closest to the customer to ensure that these ideas were wholly workable.

Information flows: the 'bottom-up' approach

Fashion companies adopting the bottom-up approach to marketing planning will be those who involve units and personnel throughout the organization. Information flows up through the organization to top management; in most cases units will prepare individual plans which will be incorporated into the main marketing plan or will contribute key information on which the plan will be based. The new management systems at Laura Ashley positively encourage this information communication channel with their '£5.00 for a good idea' scheme for staff. Although this approach can be slower than the top-down approach, it has the advantage of allowing those closest to the customer and those responsible for implementation to have a say in the process.

The planning cycle

The marketing planning cycle in the fashion industry tends to be much shorter than in other countries. Of necessity, it is governed by the cyclical nature of the seasons, companies are dealing with what is in marketing terms between two and eight new product launches in a year. It is not surprising that, in many small organizations, marketing planning can deteriorate into a series of short-term tactics.

At the other end of the scale, many of the larger retail, clothing and textile giants will be planning for the medium to long term, and the large-scale planning process can lead to unimaginative use of marketing tactics in the short term. Plans covering a short timescale of one or two seasons are termed short-range plans. Marketing plans that look ahead 2–5 years are known as medium-range plans and long-range plans are those which deal with time spans of 5 years or more. These tend to be few and far between in today's rapidly changing business environment, although the fashion retail giants, with their huge property portfolios, still need to consider the longer-term future in their marketing plans.

Whatever the timescale of the marketing plans, most well-organized firms tend to plan on a continuous basis. The widespread use of information technology has greatly improved efficiency in this field, allowing plans to be updated with ease. A typical planning cycle is shown in Figure 11.2.

For many fashion marketers, the idea of having such a system may seem anathema; without it, fashion marketing too quickly becomes

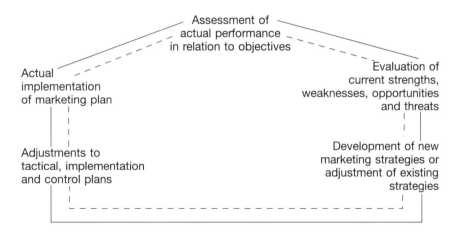

Figure 11.2 A typical marketing planning cycle
Key: —— Flow of information
        - - - Feedback loop demonstrating organic nature of planning process

product-centred, with customers' interests almost taking second place. Once the system is in place, a regular pattern soon develops, and the organization's efforts can be marshalled in one harmonious direction.

Crisis management

We have included a discussion of crisis management within the framework of this chapter on fashion marketing planning because, all too often, planning needs only become apparent when a crisis develops. A fashion company which runs on very informal lines, with the balance of effort being extended on production rather than marketing, can survive adequately while the economy is booming. When there are economic difficulties, external triggers, for example the bankruptcy of a major distributor, or internal triggers, such as a cash-flow crisis, create a need for marketing planning, by which time it is often too late to be able to gather information sufficient for an adequate decision.

NEW APPROACHES TO MARKETING PLANNING

Learning about the classic methods of marketing planning is a useful means of developing a more customer-orientated approach to fashion marketing. However, most marketing strategy experts are now coming to the conclusion that a rigid system of planning is unsuited to the turbulent business environment – a view with which many fashion marketers will empathize. Paul Fifield in this book *Marketing Strategy* (1993) broaches the topic of 'new age marketing', where he suggests that marketers will need to 'approach their marketplaces in a more "whole" manner, i.e. by blending elements of logic and emotion'. This certainly accords with some of the latest developments in fashion marketing strategy (Evans 1989) where greater emphasis is placed on the inner-directedness of the consumer, leading to longer-term brand images, in a more widely segmented market.

To some extent, fashion designers in the UK have been in the vanguard of such a process, interpreting people's moods and translating these into a look. What has been lacking in the British fashion industry has been the ability to systematize it and to translate the inspiration into a workable marketing strategy. The company which has achieved this synthesis of image and strategy is the German men's fashion clothing company Hugo Boss, which has a strong emotive brand image and a well-organized marketing strategy to back it.

STRATEGY DEVELOPMENT TOOLS FOR THE FASHION MARKETER

The starting point of many fashion marketers' plans has often been the intuitive understanding their designers have of the market. Top European companies, like Benetton and Escada, tend to use a blend of inspiration and calculation in the development of their marketing activities. Benetton, for example, used 'shock tactic' advertising which worked with their target audience. Escada ventured into the use of recycled textiles at just the right point to gain maximum exposure, but both these companies took a degree of risk in moving outside the norm. Although many companies will develop their own strategic planning methods, there are a number of tools in general use which form a useful starting point when developing a strategy.

Porter's 5-force analysis

Michael Porter (1979) put forward the idea that an industry's profitability is determined by five key factors:

- Intensity of competition between rivals
- Buyer's bargaining power
- Supplier's bargaining power
- Threat to new entrants
- Availability of substitutes

A company in an industry where buyers are weak, where there are few substitutes and high barriers to entry through costs and technology, is likely to be highly profitable, telecommunications services are a prime example. Fashion, on the other hand, is an immensely competitive industry at all levels, where buyers, both retail buyers and the consumer, are tremendously powerful, and substitutes are readily available. To be successful, fashion marketers must be able to recognize the factors and respond to the problems.

'Boston' matrix – product portfolio analysis

Understanding the business environment is only one aspect of strategy development; understanding your own organization is the other side of the coin. The Boston Consulting Group matrix provides one way of examining how strategic business units, which can be a range of companies owned by a larger group (as is the case with Burtons) or a range of products (e.g. Pretty Polly's range of hosiery), relate to one another in terms of market share and contribution to cash flow (see Figure 11.3).

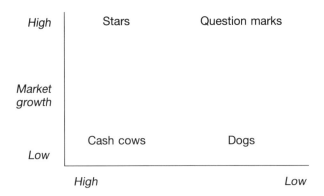

Figure 11.3 Boston matrix

A brief explanation of the terms in the Boston matrix is given below:

- **Stars**   These have a high share of a growing market, although they are still relatively new products, they require additional spending (e.g. on promotions).
- **Cash cows**   These are established products with high shares in a low-growth market, they require little additional marketing expenditure and so they generate a lot of cash for the company, they are usually classic items.
- **Question marks**   These tend to be products in a high-growth market but with a low market share. If they are to survive, they need plenty of additional expenditure.
- **Dogs**   These are potential problems – products that have a low share of a low-growth market; typically they are products that have reached the end of their product life cycle, and ideally should either be regenerated or axed from the range.

A company needs 'cash cows' if it is to survive, for they provide the income with which it can develop 'stars' to generate future profits.

Ansoff product/market matrix

An excellent aid to strategic decision making is the Ansoff product/market matrix. It allows the organization to see how its products are distributed across new and existing markets, and to identify new options (see Figure 11.4). The strategies open to the organization are as follows:

- **Market penetration**   Following this route the organization will maintain or increase its share of the existing market with its current products. This will usually be achieved through competitive pricing or increased expenditure on distribution.

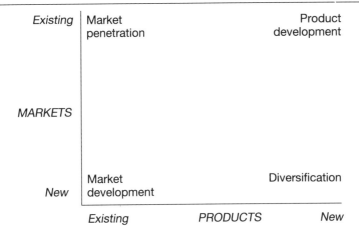

Figure 11.4 Ansoff product/market matrix

- **Market development** Here the firm seeks new markets for its existing products either through exporting or investigating new market segments.
- **Product development** This is the strategy most frequently adopted by fashion marketers, whereby new products are created for existing market segments and distribution channels.
- **Diversification** Here the firm seeks to develop new products in new markets. Few fashion companies have been able to diversify successfully without fundamentally undermining their core product. Levi's diversification into suit production and Biba's establishment of a household goods range are two salutary examples from the past.

The classic marketing planning process

An understanding of the classic marketing planning process is undeniably helpful, both in developing one's own marketing plans and in interpreting the strategies and actions of competitors. A brief outline was given earlier, now we will consider the issue in depth.

Each step as defined in Figure 11.5 will now be explained in depth.

- **Marketing audit** The marketing audit will be a thorough review of the company's situation, which will cover both the macro- and micro-environmental factors. In addition, the internal strengths and weaknesses of the company will be assessed, in particular, the financial strength, the personnel and management and, most important for the fashion company, the strength of factors like design production and all the elements of the 'marketing mix'. Marketing audits are frequently carried out by external advisers, who are able to

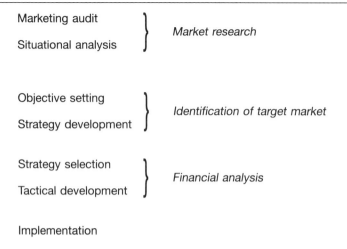

Figure 11.5 The classic marketing planning process

bring a fresh perspective to the company, though in a smaller firm the marketing manager can conduct the audit.

- **Situational analysis**   The situational analysis will be derived from examining evidence gathered by the marketing audit in terms of the internal strengths and weaknesses and the external opportunities and threats facing the company. This allows the marketing manager to assess how the company stands in relation to competitors and the marketplace; for example, in the late 1980s, Marks and Spencer had to address the fact that their differential advantage of quality was being seized by competitors.

- **Objective setting**   Objectives will be set which are achievable and in tune with the ethos of the organization. Usually these are expressed quantitatively, either in financial or market-share terms. Increasingly, there has been a trend to also set objectives in qualitative terms, Anita Roddick's Body Shop being a classic example.

- **Strategy development**   Strategy refers to the way in which an organization hopes to achieve its objectives. For example, the resurgence of the fashion for attractive underwear, spearheaded by the Burton group, meant that other underwear manufacturers needed to retain market share. Strategies for doing so utilized the 4'P's of the marketing mix, including improved design of the product, attractive packaging and advertising, together with improved relations with distributors, which enabled the manufacturers psychologically to justify increases in price. To put it simply, marketing planning strategy involves deciding in broad terms how you will use the marketing planning tools (the 4'P's) to achieve your objectives. This may mean choosing one strategy from a variety of alternatives.

- **Development of tactics**   Once the strategy has been decided, the details must be worked out and this means the tactics. When the recession began to affect the UK hosiery market in the early 1990s, leading firms such as Pretty Polly began to concentrate on developing brand names and new products as a way of retaining market share and profitability. Naturally, advertising played a large part in creating brand awareness, particularly for their new Lycra products. The decision to use advertising in this way was a strategic decision. The tactics were the details of exactly when and where the advertisements were to be shown.

- **Market research**   At each stage of the marketing planning process, market research plays a vital role. The fashion marketer will obviously use some of the marketing research tools, particularly information in issues like competition held on the MIS database, when carrying out the marketing audit. At the objective-setting stage, the marketer will use secondary research to confirm issues such as whether a market is of sufficient size to make it viable.

  It is on the level of strategy development and selection that marketing research is even more valuable to the fashion marketer. The decision to go ahead with a new product such as Lycra tights and stockings could only be made on the basis of market research to ensure that the product was acceptable to the consumer. Similarly, research is crucial to ensure that the correct tactics are successful, for instance, checking that the target market actually reads a given magazine or newspaper.

- **Identification of target market**   Knowing the target market for the product is vital in developing successful strategies and tactics. Identifying the target market requires an examination of both the market research results and the distinctive competences of the company. For example, Evans has identified the larger-sized fashion buyer as their target market, and geared their marketing strategies towards this market.

  In addition to identifying the psychographic (i.e. lifestyle) profile of the target market, the fashion marketer also needs to ensure that they have some 'hard' demographic information about this segment, for example, the likely numbers of people in the sector and the amounts of disposable and discretionary income they have. Sales forecasts must then be developed to estimate the size of the market. Only when the target market has been fully identified can strategy be worked out and tactics developed; this allows for the precision that is so important for the fashion marketer today. Hugo Boss, with their target market as the fashionably dressed European man aged 30–50 advertises heavily in *The Economist*, *GQ* and *For Men*. An advertisement for Jo Bloggs, on the other hand, would need to be placed in *Sky*, *Live Lizzard* or *Q*.

- **Financial analysis** Above all else, marketing plans must be financially viable if they are to be successful. On the basis of the sales forecasts, a budget will need to be drawn up, both for the overall marketing plan and for each individual aspect of that plan. Thus there will be a distribution plan, a promotions plan and so on, each with their own budgets. The main task for the fashion market is to work out the most cost effective method of reaching the target market within the budgetary constraints allowed.
- **Implementation** Actually putting the plan into effect requires an immense amount of organization and the co-operation of the whole team, which very often includes those outside the organization such as PR consultants. Distribution channels must be in place before promotion gets fully underway, so that the product is available to meet demand, and all quality problems with the product must be eliminated at an early stage to ensure that it meets consumer expectations.

  In the highly competitive fashion market, smooth implementation of the marketing plan is even more important than in other industries, to ensure that other firms do not have the opportunity to bring out a competing product or take advantage of gaps in distribution by offering their own alternative product.

Control

In developing the marketing plan, the control elements are put in place; control factors will be the measurement of actual performance against expected performance in areas like the budget, achievement of market shares, and so on. This comparison must be made within each individual element of the marketing plan. The feedback provided by the control process allows for the marketing plan to be adjusted, for instance, adjustments can be made to the product, or indeed, for a new set of plans to be developed.

The marketing control process in the fashion industry has been transformed by technological innovations such as EPoS, which allow immediate feedback on sales of particular designs. Developments in market research have also allowed marketers access to more sophisticated information on the consumer.

SUMMARY

Although inspirational design has an important role to play in the success of the fashion company, fashion marketers also need to use strategic planning in order to ensure the long-term survival of their organization.

The basic planning tools the fashion marketer uses are the same as in any other industry. The key difference lies in the constraints within which the fashion industry operates. It has a far shorter planning cycle, dealing with up to eight new product launches per year. As fashion is a social activity, so fashion marketing is more vulnerable to social changes than other industries.

The intensely competitive nature of the industry means that marketing planning is essential for survival and growth, particularly in the international context. The major players in the international fashion market adopt a strategic approach to marketing which enables them to capture key markets and ensures they can be ready to adapt to change far more readily than the organizations which rely entirely on intuition.

DISCUSSION POINTS

1 The fashion fur industry, which was immensely successful in the 1960s is now in seemingly terminal decline. Evaluate the factors in the marketing environment which have caused this.
2 Decide on a fashion item, it can be one of your own designs or a new design which you admire, and decide who will be the target market for that product. Draw up an outline of a marketing plan with suggested tactics for marketing your product.
3 The fashion industry has been criticized for being insufficiently 'environmentally friendly'. Discuss ways in which this criticism could be counteracted in a marketing plan.
4 Discuss ways in which the fashion marketer can overcome the problem of having such a short planning cycle.

Chapter 12

The future of fashion marketing

The main difficulty in dealing with the complex world of fashion marketing is the issue of change. Fashion, by its very nature, is constantly changing, and there is a further dimension of constant change in the business environment. Predicting exactly what changes might occur is a dangerous business, but environmental scanning is one of the major responsibilities of the marketing manager. To conclude, we have decided to take the PESTEL factors to examine where future changes may exist.

Political changes have dramatically affected the available market for the fashion industry. Once the Soviet Union was seen as a vast potential market, but the sophistication of that empire's military technology masked the fact that their consumers had very little spending power. The former USSR is likely to remain an economic backwater, in much the same way that post-colonial Africa has been, for some time to come.

Political instability in Europe could lead to change in the whole orientation of the fashion industry towards the East. The Far East itself is undergoing much restructuring; countries such as Singapore and Hong Kong are now acting as middle men sourcing manufacture from India, China and even Russia. As these countries' economies have expanded so have the aspirations of their workforces, the workforces are showing a greater preference for the retail trade rather than manufacturing. As the economy has expanded it has meant that wages and conditions have improved, making cheap manufacture impossible. Any political changes in these countries would have effects in Europe as the Far Eastern countries have access to the Australian, Chinese and Russian/Soviet markets.

In 1991 it was decided that the multi-fibre arrangement would be phased out over ten years and it is hoped that in its place the GATT arrangements will sufficiently cover matters such as dumping, subsidies and counterfeiting. The effects of any such agreements are always subject to countries' political change. However, most nations are aware of the need for such policies.

Economic changes have a profound effect on the fashion industry, especially the retail sector. The economic boom/bust cycle shows few signs of change at present. However, in an internationally competitive industry like fashion, broader economic issues need to be considered, like the relatively low economic growth of Europe as compared to the Far East, for example.

In Britain particularly, the world recession of the late 1980s and early 1990s has had a profound effect on the average consumer. Many consumers are now carrying what is termed 'negative equity' on their mortgages, that is, their property is worth less than when they bought it. Some of these people spent heavily on credit cards; they are unlikely to spend so rapidly again.

Fashion businesses have become much more cost and price conscious, they are looking at and observing the consumer more, as they cannot afford to take risks. The hope for the British fashion industry is that bodies such as the Fashion Council will promote and support it backed by government.

As other countries' economies grow they will provide a threat to the UK industry and its market. The French government has always heavily supported its fashion industry; more recently, the Spanish government made its fashion/textile industry a priority, pouring money into it to ensure its establishment across Europe; Germany, which has been at the forefront of quality manufacture of textiles and garments has seen its economy suffer with the effects of the world recession and the expansion to include the former East Germany. This could leave a gap for countries prepared to invest in new technology.

Other countries with more stable and affluent economies such as Sweden and Norway have started to promote their fashion onto the world scene. The effect of more and further production of fashion is obviously to cause the saturation and then the reduction of markets. It will be those countries whose economies are stable and who are supported by their governments that will continue to prosper economically through their industry.

Social changes have a great and obvious impact on fashion. The social revolution of the 1960s has changed the shape of the fashion industry, it has made fashion accessible to all social classes. The post-war generation has provided the innovative fashion marketer with ready markets, however, this group is fickle. Having once decided that the creations of Bodymap were too avant-garde they then decided that Next was too bland. At the end of the 1980s they also decided that materialism was bad and that they did not want to be sold to. The correct image is very important for this, the largest-spending consumer group, disliking as they do any labels such as 'mum', 'housewife', etc.

The clothing industry will have to rethink classification systems if it is to benefit from these markets. As expectations have changed, people have wanted to accomplish more. This is not just with regard to their employment, but also in the way they live. Sport and leisure have become very important to the fashion industry. Sports- and casual-wear has become acceptable day wear, not just for the young but across ages and classes. This has been due to a growing informality; today it is rare to dress for the theatre or to go to a restaurant as was expected 20 years ago. Travel has become important, people are travelling further afield, with America and the Far East becoming popular destinations. As a population has experienced more, they have also demanded more at home.

Now that the iconoclastic youth of the 1960s are becoming the older generation, fashion marketers are adopting a different approach. This generation has been accustomed to spending on fashion, and, indeed, the over 50s, whose children have grown up, have more disposable income and see fashion as appropriate to spend their money on. To date, fashion marketers have coped with this change by extending the 'young, non-teen' market segment through to age 45. However, it is likely that fashions will adapt to make them attractive for the older consumer too.

Increased mobility through greater ownership of transport has meant a move away from towns as workers are able to commute to work. This has had two main effects: it has meant that the high street in cities and towns has declined, while out of town developments, such as Thurrock, Lakeside have increased. It is in these developments that the multiple chain stores have found new markets, however, it will be some time before an accurate assessment can be determined concerning their profitability. Retailers are also looking for new sites. For example, the success of outlets at railway stations has seen new retail expansion into airports.

Consumer movements have also enabled the development of mail order as shoppers have become less interested in spending Saturdays 'in town'. Those stores in town have had to adapt, many now operate late-night shopping once a week. They have also been keen to offer the consumer Sunday shopping.

Technological change has already altered many aspects of fashion marketing. Improvements in manufacturing techniques have meant that production can take place in almost any part of the world. Systems such as FabricSave, PressRite, TeamSim and Apparel Vision Stitch are reducing the costs of manufacture and training.

Technological change has also begun to affect marketing methods. Computer power has meant that micro-market segmentation has become a reality. Some retailers are now using systems similar to 'Spaceman' operated by Boots. This not only calculates what items are selling well, but at what times they sell, it also observes where they sell best. Using these systems sales staff could move stock around to maximize potential sales.

Marks and Spencer is now using videos at the sales counter to promote goods and special offers to customers waiting in queues. This technique is likely to be widely copied, most people will be familiar with its usage at the Post Office.

The growth in direct marketing is set to continue, especially on an international basis. Coupled with technological innovations in design and manufacturing, 'customized' mass market products could be available soon.

Littlewoods is developing home shopping through television channels. As the usage of satellite and cable television increases, other retailers especially mail order concerns, could find that this is a viable option. It does have to be noted that for many consumers the actual shopping is part of the experience, they enjoy going into different shops, trying on goods, and so on. It may be the case that if this 'pleasure' is removed then those consumers may not be enticed to purchase as much.

New fabrics are continually being developed, many of these are produced with both ecological and environmental concerns in mind such as Novotex 'green cotton' and Junichi Arai fabrics. Some fashion fads never really take off initially, e.g. disposable paper clothes, which are presently only used in hospitals. However, further techniques are beginning to suggest that paper clothing may yet be a viable mass market option.

One of the noticeable aspects of the post-war generation has been their ability to protest. These were the groups who protested during the 1960s and 1970s over various issues such as women's rights, Vietnam and nuclear weapons. They were not always taken seriously, but today they have been given a new recognition. They are able to protest in a way that industry and government understands, that is, with their purses and their votes. They have done this recently in showing their concern for the environment. The marketers were not far behind and the marketing of caring became a profitable industry.

In a Mintel report of April 1988 it was declared that being seen to be green was good for business. The green industry expanded rapidly and the term 'environmentally friendly' became a catchphrase for profit. Originally the fashion industry was in a dilemma; there was a valuable market but at a time of recession, investment was considered too costly. Today many environmentally friendly textiles are being produced, some fashion companies have adopted environmental policies which include the usage of a percentage of recycled fibre in their product base. Synthetics have again come of age.

The charity industry has not escaped this new altruistic mood, and the fact is that many of them are involved in the promotion of good environmental practice. They have understood the need for marketing and realized the need for a professional approach overall. Many charity

Plate 12.1 Courtaulds new Tencil 'Denim' fabric (dress by Helen Storey)

shops dealing in second-hand clothing employ merchandisers to help staff understand how to present clothes and also to recognize the value of a designer label. Oxfam have started their NO LOGO shops, where better quality second-hand goods are offered.

Traidcraft not only buys goods from the Third World but, like Oxfam, has helped to develop co-operatives which produce goods for sale across Europe. They have learnt to pick up on trends such as the ethnic look and to take advantage of changing social awareness and behaviour, i.e. consumers are more likely to buy goods if they feel they are helping others. This forms a small part of what can be regarded as world ecological economics, but clearly it represents a set of priorities that will continue to be high on the consumer's mind.

Legal issues will still continue to affect the fashion industry. Europe and the US have strict controls regarding information to the consumer of care of the fabric. With further developments in the environmental concerns of fashion production it could be that existing laws could be extended.

The single European market is likely to have the largest impact on the fashion industry. Maastricht and the social charter is an issue which will never have all the European members in agreement, however, the outcome of it will have a bearing on the manufacture and retail of fashion in Europe. This is particularly true with regard to directives such as those covering health and safety and minimum wages. The textile industry benefits from the European Commission which provides funding for research, it is likely that many of these projects will continue to develop, ensuring that the industry has access to developing technology.

Above all, the most important factor in fashion marketing is that we are now seeing a highly discerning, knowledgeable consumer who is aware of quality and price. This consumer knowledge spans across all ages and, in the UK, classes. Children today are very fashion conscious and are encouraged to be so by their peers, television and other media and occasionally their parents! However, the media also feeds them other images making them aware of environmental and ecological issues. They are less likely to want goods with negative associations and will influence their parents as to consumer purchases.

Fashion marketers are going to have to prepare themselves for much greater segmentation of markets and not just rely on vague stereotypes to classify a market such as the menswear market for those aged 25–40. In the late 1980s the 'new' man, seduced by images of himself, spent money on items he had not generally considered before, such as cosmetics, toiletries and magazines. The fact that this was new meant that purchasing happened. During the expansion of the menswear market another market was noted. It was referred to as 'the pink pound' as marketers recognized that gay men had large amounts of disposable income.

In the future all markets need to be examined much more closely in order to ensure consumer interest. The 'grey' market is no longer new and it will not be long before the post-war generation will reach retirement age. UK marketers will have to position themselves to provide for all segments of this generation as well as exploring new opportunities with the younger markets.

In the minds of the consumer the concept of fashion has also changed; it is now worn by all, young and old. Size is no longer the barrier it once was. Although statistics had been coming to the same conclusion that, in general, people are becoming larger it took the UK industry longer to catch on than its US and European counterparts. Now, however, Harrods has opened a whole department catering for larger sizes, Hennes have their own larger range, Dawn French and designer Helen Teague formed the company 1647 and many more are likely to emerge.

Retailers have devised many marketing and selling strategies. The most popular strategy has been to trade out the recession. Those companies who established themselves in the 1980s and have managed to acquire a staying power are now well placed to continue. There were those who predicted that Next would be no more in 1990, yet in 1993 it announced profits when many of its competitors were still announcing losses.

In this book we have concentrated on the marketing process. However, this process would not take place were it not for the designers of the fashions and textiles. Their constant production of new and exciting ideas, their commitment to the consumer, whether couture, ready-to-wear or high street, ensures that the fashion marketer remains in business.

Select bibliography

The bibliography given here is not exhaustive, but it provides an indication of the reading that students may wish to pursue if they want to follow up either the marketing topics or any industry-specific material.

Ansoff, H.I. (1988) *The New Corporate Strategy*, Wiley.

Cannon, Tom (1992) *Basic Marketing*, Cassell.

Curran, L. (1991) 'Theories of Fashion and the Euro-Consumer', *Hollings Apparel Industry Review*, 8(2): pp. 39–60.

Dibb, Simkin, Pride and Ferrell (1991) *Marketing*, Houghton Mifflin.

Economist Intelligence Unit (1991) *The Clothing Industry and The Single European Market*.

Economist Intelligence Unit (1992) *Textiles and Clothing In Eastern Europe*.

Evans, Martin (1989) 'Consumer Behaviour Towards Fashion', *European Journal of Marketing* (1989) 23:7.

Fifield Paul (1993) *Marketing Strategy*, Heinemann.

Gold, Annalee (1976) *How to Sell Fashion*, Dryden.

Hook, Sallie (1987) 'Managers Must Know the Conceptual Distinctions of Fashion Marketing' *Marketing News*, 21: 10.

Katz and Lazarfeld (1955) *Personal Influence*, New York: Free Press.

Knee, D. and Walters, D. (1985) *Strategy in Retailing: Theory and Application*, P. Allan.

Midgley, D.K. (1974) 'Innovation in the Male Fashion Market: The Parallel Diffusion Hypothesis', *ESOMAR Fashion Research and Marketing*, Dec.

Murphy and Staples (1979) 'A Modernised Family Life Cycle', *Journal of Consumer Research*, June.

Porter, M. (1979) 'How Competitive Forces Shape Strategy', *Harvard Business Review* Mar/Apr.

Sanghavi, Witin, (1987) 'Customer Service', *Retail and Distribution*, Nov.

Terpstra, V. (1987) *International Marketing*, Dryden, 1987.

TMS Partnership (1993) *British Clothing Market Overview*.

Ward, Scott (1972) 'Children's Reactions to Commercials', *Journal of Advertising Research*, April.

Winters A.A. and Goodman, S. (1984) *Fashion Sales Promotion* New York: FIT.

Appendix I

USEFUL ADDRESSES

British Fashion Council
7 Swallow Place
London W1R 7AA
Tel: 071 408 0020

Chartered Institute of Marketing
Moor Hall
Cookham
Berkshire
SL6 9QH
Tel: 0628 524922

Appendix II

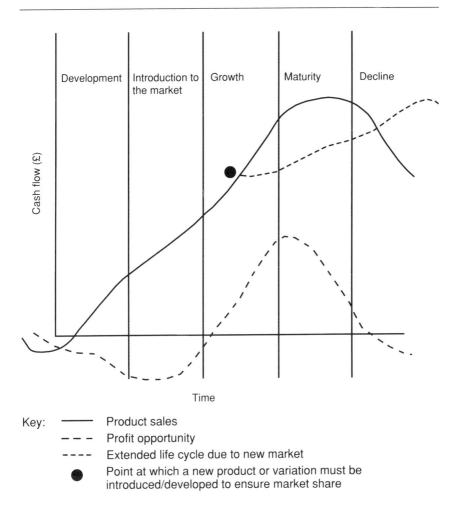

Development | Introduction to the market | Growth | Maturity | Decline

Cash flow (£)

Time

Key:
—— Product sales
- - - Profit opportunity
---- Extended life cycle due to new market
● Point at which a new product or variation must be introduced/developed to ensure market share

Figure A.1 Fashion product life cycle

Index